LENT, HOLY WEEK, EASTER

LENT
HOLY WEEK
EASTER

SERVICES AND PRAYERS

Commended by the House of Bishops of
the General Synod of the Church of England

CHURCH HOUSE PUBLISHING
CAMBRIDGE UNIVERSITY PRESS
SPCK

The copyright in *Lent, Holy Week, Easter: Services and Prayers* is held by
the Central Board of Finance of the Church of England.

Copyright © The Central Board of Finance of the Church of England 1984, 1986.

For further information about copyright see p. 300

Designed and printed in Great Britain at Cambridge University Press
Set in Monophoto Bembo by Servis Filmsetting Ltd.

Jointly published by

Church House Publishing
Church House, Great Smith Street, London SW1P 3NZ

Cambridge University Press
The Edinburgh Building, Shaftesbury Road, Cambridge CB2 2RU

SPCK: The Society for Promoting Christian Knowledge
Holy Trinity Church, Marylebone Road, London NW1 4DU

British Library Cataloguing in Publication Data
Lent, Holy Week, Easter: services and prayers.
1. Church of England–Liturgy–Texts
2. Holy Week–Liturgy–Texts   3. Lent–Liturgy–Texts
I. Title
264'.035   BX5147.H6

ISBN   0 7151 37050 0 (Church House Publishing)
         0 521 50701 4 (Cambridge University Press)
         0 281 04204 7 (SPCK)

★

CONTENTS

LENT, HOLY WEEK, EASTER
SERVICES AND PRAYERS

These Services and Prayers have been commended by the House of Bishops of the General Synod and are published with the agreement of the House.

Under Canon B 4 it is open to each Bishop to authorize, if he sees fit, the form of service to be used within his diocese. He may specify that the services shall be those commended by the House, or that a diocesan form of them shall be used. If the Bishop gives no directions in this matter the priest remains free, subject to the terms of Canon B 5, to make use of the Services as commended by the House.

On behalf of the House of Bishops

ROBERT CANTUAR:
Chairman

INTRODUCTION

The services here presented were composed in response to an instruction from the House of Bishops to the Liturgical Commission.

The Commission began by attempting to analyse the needs of the Church. These are so varied that it passes the wit of man to provide for them all. Nor would it be necessary to do so; for there must always be a place for initiative and experiment. The prompting of the Holy Spirit is not restricted to liturgical forms. The forms of the future are worked out here and there in imaginative parishes. It is not our purpose to lay a monolithic and inflexible order upon the Church of England. Indeed there are many who question the wisdom of this undertaking. Let the parishes carry on with their existing freedom, borrowing from Rome or the Joint Liturgical Group or doing what they have always done! But precisely because there is variety and some uncertainty, it seems prudent to chart a viable course through the competing orders. The early evidence of the diocesan liturgical secretaries and the subsequent enthusiastic approval of the Church at large point firmly in this direction. For our part we are content that these services shall take their place according to their intrinsic merit.

This collection has certain characteristics which make it potentially useful to our people. First, the services are closely tailored to the ASB. The degree of acceptance achieved by the ASB is in many ways astounding. The Church is learning to use that book and still needs a period of assimilation before revision is attempted. It would be greatly to the Church's benefit if the experience of the ASB were widened to include the services here presented. Second, they are more than a few services collected together. We are providing a *directory* from which choices may be made. We think of this book as a manual to be used with selectivity, sensitivity and imagination. Not least important are the lections. At the same time we have set out the services so that they *may* be used as they stand.

Nevertheless there are some things we have not done. We have not provided alternative versions of services for use with the Book of Common Prayer. This was our original intention, but we abandoned it because it became evident that, by and large, those using the Book of Common Prayer on the occasions envisaged do not require this kind of provision. On the other hand, with judicious adaptation, almost everything in this book can be used with Rite B. Of course the Book of Common Prayer can be enriched by the splendid work of Eric Milner-White in *My God My Glory* and *A Procession of Passion Prayers*. We have not sought to provide services for each day in Holy Week. The attempt to relate each day to events in the last week of the Lord's life is not wholly successful. Those who desire this close synchronization may turn to the JLG *Holy Week Services* or compose their own services from the directory.

Again, we have not sought to be innovative. The time to introduce that which departs from traditional usages is when new experiments have already been tested and won approval. Liturgy is essentially conservative because of the nature of the Church as a historical body founded in Scripture. The Holy Spirit takes the things of Christ and shows them unto us. Worship has a dimension of directness but also a dimension of history and tradition. Our worship is one with the worship of the whole Church of the ages. To be a Christian is to enter into the tradition consciously and gladly. Our task has been to distil from the experience of the past the forms appropriate to the present and to present them in the idioms of the present.

This is a theological perception of some importance. We have aimed to preserve the proper continuity with the past, but with freshness. Liturgy is not something we 'make up', nor is tradition a musty past to be left behind by modern pioneers. On the contrary, tradition is nothing less than the inner life of the Church. It is received, participated in . . . it is the life of the Holy Spirit in the Church. In this connection we draw attention to the place of silence in these services, conscious that silence is of more pervasive importance as the sign of our participation in the tradition.

A related consequence of this perception is that we have distanced ourselves from every attempt simply to reconstruct past events. This is of special importance in these services, where the temptation is strong to encourage an imaginative representation of the events in our Lord's life. We do not think of assisting worshippers by mental effort to go back to the first Palm Sunday and Good Friday. We think of assisting them to make a present liturgical celebration. The cross and the resurrection are inseparable. It is in the light of the resurrection that we worship the Crucified Lord and are united with him. To enter into the tradition is to stand in the divine presence. Here we are most conscious that we have not always succeeded. It may be that the rest is a matter of presentation. Certainly the services will be nothing until they are presented, and presentation must involve the theological perception we have discussed here in both presenters and congregation.

The notes have been compiled with care, and among them will be found hints to facilitate presentation. We would wish to draw the attention of those who skip quickly through these pages to the need for attention to these notes. Some of the services we have ourselves tried out with a congregation. We found out what we ought to have known. The service on the printed page is one thing. The service *prayed* is literally another world. The notes do something to indicate the reality of worship. In particular there were members of the Commission who had reservations about providing for an *agape*. But everyone who participated in it was deeply moved and felt its validity.

It will quickly become plain to those who study and use these services that there is considerable scope for the skill and inspiration of composers. We have not thought it right to commission musical settings. The best does not always come to order. But we would draw the attention of composers to the Good Friday anthem, the psalms (which cry out for

3

congregational and responsorial chants), the Exsultet, the Old Testament canticles, and to the need for seasonal settings of Holy Communion. Of course the old should sometimes be used. But there is great need for the new. The Christian community sings – from inner necessity it sings.

DOUGLAS JONES
Chairman of the Liturgical Commission

GENERAL NOTES

1. **Options within the Services**   The services in *Lent, Holy Week, Easter* are set out so that they may be used as they stand. Alternatively, they may be used as source material for locally produced services. The symbol ▶ indicates sections which are integral to the services as conceived by those who wrote them. Every part of these services is optional other than the mandatory sections of Holy Communion Rite A.

   Texts in bold type are to be said by the congregation.

2. **Saying and Singing**   Where rubrics indicate that a section is to be 'said', this must be understood to include 'or sung' and vice versa.

3. **Posture**   Wherever a certain posture is particularly appropriate, it is indicated in the left-hand margin. At all other points local custom may be established and followed.

4. **Traditional Texts**   Where parts of a service are sung to well-known settings, the traditional words for which they were composed may be used.

5. **Holy Communion Rite B**   In any services combined with the Holy Communion the equivalent texts from Rite B may be used in place of those provided here for Rite A.

6. **The Lord's Prayer**   On any occasion the Lord's Prayer may be used in its modern form (as in Holy Communion Rite A), or in its modified form (as in Holy Communion Rite B), or in its traditional form (as in the Book of Common Prayer).

7. **Hymns**   Various points are indicated for the singing of hymns: but, if occasion requires, they may be sung at other points also.

8. **The President at the Holy Communion**   The president (who, in accordance with the provisions of Canon B 12 'Of the ministry of the Holy Communion', must have been episcopally ordained priest) presides over the whole of the service. At the eucharist he says the opening Greeting, the Collect, the Absolution, the Peace, and the

Blessing; he himself must take the bread and the cup before replacing them on the holy table, say the Eucharistic Prayer, break the consecrated bread, and receive the sacrament on every occasion. The remaining parts of the service he may delegate to others.

When the Bishop is present, he should be president.

9 **The Minister** It is appropriate that the Imposition of Ashes, the Procession of Palms, and the Service of Light (together with the Renewal of Baptismal Vows) should normally be combined with the Holy Communion. However, when a priest is not available, these services are combined with a Ministry of the Word, and a deacon or lay person may preside. Similarly a deacon or lay person may preside on Good Friday.

10 **Kyrie Eleison** This may be used in English or Greek and in any form authorized by the ASB. During Lent and Holy Week it may be replaced by the Trisagion (for texts see pp. 285–286).

11 **The Collect** The Collect may be introduced by the words 'Let us pray' and a brief bidding, after which silence may be kept.

12 **Lectionary** A lectionary (p. 294) is provided for the main Holy Days in these seasons, including a continuous cycle from Palm Sunday to the First Sunday after Easter. Psalms and readings from this lectionary are recommended for use with these services. Alternatively, any of the authorized lectionaries may be used. Sentences, psalms and readings may be read in any authorized version.

13 **Psalms** The psalms provided for the Holy Communion are closely related to the readings and should be used. The gradual psalm (that is, the psalm which follows the first reading) is provided with a response which may be used at the beginning, after each verse or group of verses, and at the end. The points at which responses may be said are indicated by **R** 'Glory to the Father . . .' is not added to the gradual psalm. If the psalms are sung to Anglican chants, the responses are not used.

14 **Acclamations in the Eucharistic Prayer** These are optional. They may be introduced by the president with the words 'Let us proclaim the mystery of faith' or with other suitable words, or they

may be used without introduction. Alternative Acclamations are
suggested.

15 **The Distribution of Holy Communion**   The following words
of distribution may be used.
    At the giving of the bread
      The bread of heaven in Christ Jesus.
    At the giving of the cup
      The blood of Christ, the cup of life.
The communicant replies **Amen**.
Any other authorized words of distribution may be used.

LENT

LENT

AN ORDER FOR
THE BEGINNING OF LENT

INTRODUCTION

The origin of the season of Lent lies not in any conscious re-enactment of our Lord's time in the wilderness, which remains only a secondary theme of the season, but in the rigorous preparation of Christians for the celebration of the death and resurrection of Christ in Holy Week and at Easter. The observance of Lent was at first undertaken by the baptismal candidates, for whom it was the final part of their preparation before initiation into the Church in the Easter liturgy, and by those who had been excommunicated for grave and public sin and would be readmitted to the Church's sacramental life in time for Easter after a period of penance. It was not long before the Church realized the benefit to all Christians of joining these particular categories of people in a season of preparation marked by penitence expressed in prayer and fasting. It is this sense of preparation, and so of eager expectation with Good Friday and Easter Day always in view, that should characterize the season of Lent.

The popular idea of 'giving things up' in Lent, however inadequately it is often understood, has its liturgical expression in the stark simplicity of Lenten worship. In part this is to express a spirit of penitence. But it is also in order to provide striking contrast with the joyful celebration of Easter. This 'giving up' traditionally includes the omission of the Gloria in Excelsis at the eucharist, the absence of flowers from the church, the restrained use of the organ to accompany worship, and the careful selection of texts (for instance of hymns) to avoid the use of the word 'Alleluia' and similar expressions of joy which will greet the resurrection on Easter Day. These are only examples of how a distinctive atmosphere can be introduced into the worship of the season. Priest and people must aim at an austerity that is quite different from dreariness.

The spirit of the season is also expressed by a restraint in the observance of Holy Days that interrupt the Lent ethos. The feast days of St Joseph and the Annunciation are legitimate intrusions, appropriately marked by the return of the Gloria and other signs of festival. But the lesser commemorations, except where they have particular local significance, are best observed only by inclusion in the prayers of intercession.

There has also grown up a custom of 'veiling' crosses (and, in some churches, statues also) either for the whole of Lent or from Palm Sunday. In part this development has been a misunderstanding of an early custom. What was being veiled was not the cross but the splendour of rich and jewelled metalwork. To obscure the cross in Lent and Holy Week is misplaced, though the substitution of a simple wooden cross or crucifix for a more colourful or expensive one might be an impressive symbol, and the removal of banners and pictures could enhance the atmosphere of Lent.

The order given for Ash Wednesday (with an indication that it might be used instead on the First Sunday in Lent) seeks to provide a service characterized by silence, reflection, and penitence. The service is set out in a form which combines it with the eucharist, although it may be used independently. The traditional practice of imposition of ashes is included, but the rite may profitably be used even when this custom is not followed. The service is designed not only to mark a special day but to start the local Christian congregation off on a path that can be seen, even at this early stage, to be leading to the Good Friday and Easter celebrations. Its emphasis is therefore as much on the season it inaugurates as on the day it marks.

NOTES

1   **Occasions for Use**   This service is intended primarily for use on Ash Wednesday. Where this is not possible it may be used on the First Sunday in Lent.

2   **The Litany**   The Litany at section 14 may be used at section 4. Where it is so used, the texts printed at section 46 A are not used.

3   **Silence**   The time of silence at section 15 is an integral part of the rite and should not be omitted or reduced to a mere pause.

4   **Confession**   The forms printed in Holy Communion Rite A (sections 7, 27, and 80) may be used instead of that provided here at section 16.

5   **Absolution**   Either section 20 or 21 should be included if there is no Imposition of Ashes. If there is an Imposition of Ashes both may be omitted.

6   **The Ash,** which may be used at sections 17 and 18, is by tradition the ash of the burned palms from the previous Palm Sunday, but other provision may be made.

7   **Imposition of Ashes**   The president may be assisted by others. Where there is a large congregation, it is better that several assist the president than that the words at section 18 be abbreviated. Nevertheless the president may, if necessity dictates, use only one of the two sentences at section 18 or impose ashes in silence.

8   **The Liturgical Colour** for this service is violet or Lent array.

AN ORDER FOR
THE BEGINNING OF LENT

THE PREPARATION

1   At the entry of the ministers THIS SENTENCE may be used.

> The sacrifice of God is a broken spirit: a broken
> and contrite heart you will not despise.
> *Psalm 51.17*

A HYMN, A CANTICLE, or A PSALM may be sung.

▶ 2   The president welcomes the people.

> Grace, mercy, and peace from God our Father
> and the Lord Jesus Christ be with you all
>
> **All**   **and also with you.**

▶ 3   In these or other suitable words, the president explains the
meaning of Lent and invites the people to observe it
faithfully.

> Brothers and sisters in Christ: since early days
> Christians have observed with great devotion the
> time of our Lord's passion and resurrection. It
> became the custom of the Church to prepare for
> this by a season of penitence and fasting.

> At first this season of Lent was observed by those
> who were preparing for Baptism at Easter and by
> those who were to be restored to the Church's
> fellowship from which they had been separated
> through sin. In course of time the Church came
> to recognize that, by a careful keeping of these
> days, all Christians might take to heart the call to
> repentance and the assurance of forgiveness
> proclaimed in the gospel, and so grow in faith
> and in devotion to our Lord.

I invite you, therefore, in the name of the
Church, to the observance of a holy Lent, by self-
examination and repentance; by prayer, fasting,
and self-denial; and by reading and meditating
on God's holy word.

4   KYRIE ELEISON or THE TRISAGION (see pp. 285–286) or
     THE LITANY at section 14 may be used.

▶ 5   The president says THE COLLECT.

Let us pray for grace to keep Lent faithfully.

Almighty and everlasting God
you hate nothing that you have made
and forgive the sins of all those who are penitent.
Create and make in us new and contrite hearts,
that, lamenting our sins
    and acknowledging our wretchedness,
we may receive from you, the God of all mercy,
perfect forgiveness and peace;
through Jesus Christ our Lord,
who is alive and reigns with you and the
    Holy Spirit,
one God, now and for ever.   **Amen.**

THE MINISTRY OF THE WORD

▶ 6   Either two or three readings from scripture follow. The Old
       Testament reading and the Gospel are always read, but the
       New Testament reading may be omitted.

▶ 7   **Sit**
       OLD TESTAMENT READING

Isaiah 58.1-8 TEV

The Lord says, 'Shout as loud as you can! Tell my people
Israel about their sins! They worship me every day, claiming
that they are eager to know my ways and obey my laws.

15

They say they want me to give them just laws and that they take pleasure in worshipping me.'

The people ask, 'Why should we fast if the Lord never notices? Why should we go without food if he pays no attention?'

The Lord says to them, 'The truth is that at the same time as you fast, you pursue your own interests and oppress your workers. Your fasting makes you violent, and you quarrel and fight. Do you think this kind of fasting will make me listen to your prayers? When you fast, you make yourselves suffer; you bow your heads low like a blade of grass, and spread out sackcloth and ashes to lie on. Is that what you call fasting? Do you think I will be pleased with that?

'The kind of fasting I want is this: Remove the chains of oppression and the yoke of injustice, and let the oppressed go free. Share your food with the hungry and open your homes to the homeless poor. Give clothes to those who have nothing to wear, and do not refuse to help your own relatives.

'Then my favour will shine on you like the morning sun, and your wounds will be quickly healed. I will always be with you to save you; my presence will protect you on every side.'

or *Joel 2.12–17 RSV*

'Yet even now,' says the Lord,
'return to me with all your heart,
with fasting, with weeping, and with mourning;
and rend your hearts and not your garments.'
Return to the Lord, your God,
for he is gracious and merciful,
slow to anger, and abounding in steadfast love,
and repents of evil.
Who knows whether he will not turn and repent,
and leave a blessing behind him,

a cereal offering and a drink offering
for the Lord, your God?

Blow the trumpet in Zion;
sanctify a fast;
call a solemn assembly;
gather the people.
Sanctify the congregation;
assemble the elders;
gather the children,
even nursing infants.
Let the bridegroom leave his room
and the bride her chamber.

Between the vestibule and the altar
let the priests, the ministers of the Lord, weep
and say, 'Spare your people, O Lord,
and make not your heritage a reproach,
a byword among the nations.
Why should they say among the peoples,
"Where is their God?"'

or *Amos 5.6–15 NEB*

If you would live, resort to the Lord,
or he will break out against Joseph like fire,
fire which will devour Israel with no one to quench it;
he who made the Pleiades and Orion,
who turned darkness into morning
and darkened day into night,
who summoned the waters of the sea
and poured them over the earth,
who makes Taurus rise after Capella
and Taurus set hard on the rising of the Vintager–
he who does this, his name is the Lord.
You that turn justice upside down
and bring righteousness to the ground,
you that hate a man who brings the wrongdoer to court
and loathe him who speaks the whole truth:

for all this, because you levy taxes on the poor
and extort a tribute of grain from them,
though you have built houses of hewn stone,
you shall not live in them,
though you have planted pleasant vineyards,
you shall not drink wine from them.
For I know how many your crimes are
and how countless your sins,
you who persecute the guiltless, hold men to ransom
and thrust the destitute out of court.
At that time, therefore, a prudent man will stay quiet,
for it will be an evil time.

Seek good and not evil,
that you may live,
that the Lord the God of Hosts may be firmly on your side,
as you say he is.
Hate evil and love good;
enthrone justice in the courts;
it may be that the Lord the God of Hosts
will be gracious to the survivors of Joseph.

At the end the reader may say

This is the word of the Lord.
All   **Thanks be to God.**

8   *Psalm 51.1–17*

This response may be used.

**Have mercy on us, O Lord,
for we have sinned.**

1   Have mercy on me O God in your en⏐during⏐
      goodness:
       according to the fullness of your compassion⏐ ⌣
       blot out⏐ my of⏐fences.

2 Wash me thoroughly | from my | wickedness:
   and | cleanse me | from my | sin.

3 For I acknowledge | my re | bellion:
   and my | sin is | ever · be | fore me.   **R**

4 Against you only have I sinned
     and done what is evil | in your | eyes:
   so you will be just in your sentence
   and | blameless | in your | judging.

5 Surely in wickedness I was | brought to | birth:
   and in | sin my | mother · con | ceived me.   **R**

6 You that desire truth in the | inward | parts:
   O teach me wisdom in the secret | places | of the |
   heart.

7 Purge me with hyssop and I | shall be | clean:
   wash me and I | shall be | whiter · than | snow.   **R**

8 Make me hear of | joy and | gladness:
   let the bones which | you have | broken ·
   re | joice.

9 Hide your | face · from my | sins:
   and | blot out | all · my in | iquities.   **R**

10 Create in me a clean | heart O | God:
   and re | new a · right | spirit · with | in me.

11 Do not cast me | out · from your | presence:
   do not take your | holy | spirit | from me.   **R**

12 O give me the gladness of your | help a | gain:
   and sup | port me · with a | willing | spirit.

13 Then will I teach trans | gressors · your | ways:
   and sinners shall | turn to | you a | gain.   **R**

14 O Lord God of my salvation   de | liver me · from |
   bloodshed:
   and my | tongue shall | sing of · your | righteousness.

15 O Lord | open · my | lips:
    and my | mouth · shall pro | claim your | praise.   **R**

16 You take no pleasure in sacrifice or | I would | give it:
    burnt- | offerings · you | do not | want.

17 The sacrifice of God is a | broken | spirit:
    a broken and contrite heart O God | you will |
    not de | spise.   **R**

9   NEW TESTAMENT READING (EPISTLE)

1 Corinthians 9.24-end NEB

You know (do you not?) that at the sports all the runners run
the race, though only one wins the prize. Like them, run to
win! But every athlete goes into strict training. They do it to
win a fading wreath; we, a wreath that never fades. For my
part, I run with a clear goal before me; I am like a boxer who
does not beat the air; I bruise my own body and make it
know its master, for fear that after preaching to others
I should find myself rejected.

or 2 Corinthians 5.20 – 6.2 RSV

So we are ambassadors for Christ, God making his appeal
through us. We beseech you on behalf of Christ, be
reconciled to God. For our sake he made him to be sin who
knew no sin, so that in him we might become the
righteousness of God.

Working together with him, then, we entreat you not to
accept the grace of God in vain. For he says,
  'At the acceptable time I have listened to you,
  and helped you on the day of salvation.'
Behold, now is the acceptable time; behold now is the day of
salvation.

or James 4.1-10 JB

Where do these wars and battles between yourselves first
start? Isn't it precisely in the desires fighting inside your own
selves? You want something and you haven't got it; so you
are prepared to kill. You have an ambition that you cannot
satisfy; so you fight to get your way by force. Why you don't
have what you want is because you don't pray for it; when
you do pray and don't get it, it is because you have not
prayed properly, you have prayed for something to indulge
your own desires.

You are as unfaithful as adulterous wives; don't you realize
that making the world your friend is making God your
enemy? Anyone who chooses the world for his friend turns
himself into God's enemy. Surely you don't think scripture is
wrong when it says: the spirit which he sent to live in us
wants us for himself alone? But he has been even more
generous to us, as scripture says: 'God opposes the proud but
he gives generously to the humble.' Give in to God, then;
resist the devil, and he will run away from you. The nearer
you go to God, the nearer he will come to you. Clean your
hands, you sinners, and clear your minds, you waverers.
Look at your wretched condition, and weep for it in misery;
be miserable instead of laughing, gloomy instead of happy.
Humble yourselves before the Lord and he will lift you up.

At the end the reader may say

This is the word of the Lord.

All   **Thanks be to God.**

10   A CANTICLE, A HYMN, or A PSALM may be used.

► 11   **Stand**
       THE GOSPEL

       When it is announced

All   **Glory to Christ our Saviour.**

Matthew 6.1-6, 16-18 NEB

Jesus said, 'Be careful not to make a show of your religion
before men; if you do, no reward awaits you in your Father's
house in heaven.

'Thus, when you do some act of charity, do not announce it
with a flourish of trumpets, as the hypocrites do in
synagogue and in the streets to win admiration from men.
I tell you this: they have their reward already. No; when you
do some act of charity, do not let your left hand know what
your right is doing; your good deed must be secret, and your
Father who sees what is done in secret will reward you.

'Again, when you pray, do not be like the hypocrites; they
love to say their prayers standing up in synagogue and at the
street–corners, for everyone to see them. I tell you this: they
have their reward already.

'So too when you fast, do not look gloomy like the
hypocrites: they make their faces unsightly so that other
people may see that they are fasting. I tell you this: they have
their reward already. But when you fast, anoint your head
and wash your face, so that men may not see that you are
fasting, but only your Father who is in the secret place; and
your Father who sees what is secret will give you your
reward.'

or *Matthew 6.16-21 NEB*

Jesus said, 'When you fast, do not look gloomy like the
hypocrites: they make their faces unsightly so that other
people may see that they are fasting. I tell you this: they have
their reward already. But when you fast, anoint your head
and wash your face, so that men may not see that you are

fasting, but only your Father who is in the secret place; and your Father who sees what is secret will give you your reward.

'Do not store up for yourselves treasure on earth, where it grows rusty and moth-eaten, and thieves break in to steal it. Store up treasure in heaven, where there is no moth and no rust to spoil it, no thieves to break in and steal. For where your treasure is, there will your heart be also.'

or Luke 18.9-14 NEB

Jesus told a parable, which was aimed at those who were sure of their own goodness and looked down on everyone else. 'Two men went up to the temple to pray, one a Pharisee and the other a tax gatherer. The Pharisee stood up and prayed thus: "I thank thee, O God, that I am not like the rest of men, greedy, dishonest, adulterous; or, for that matter, like this tax gatherer. I fast twice a week; I pay tithes on all that I get." But the other kept his distance and would not even raise his eyes to heaven, but beat upon his breast, saying, "O God, have mercy on me, sinner that I am." It was this man, I tell you, and not the other, who went home acquitted of his sins. For everyone who exalts himself will be humbled; and whoever humbles himself will be exalted.'

At the end the reader says

	This is the Gospel of Christ.
All	**Praise to Christ our Lord.**

▶ 12 **Sit**
THE SERMON

THE LITURGY OF PENITENCE

▶ 13 President Let us now call to mind our sin and the infinite mercy of God.

14 **Kneel**

THIS LITANY may follow if it has not already been used at section 4.

God the Father,
have mercy on us.

God the Son,
have mercy on us.

God the Holy Spirit,
have mercy on us.

Holy, blessed, and glorious Trinity,
have mercy on us.

From all evil and mischief;
from pride, vanity, and hypocrisy;
from envy, hatred, and malice;
and from all evil intent,
Good Lord, deliver us.

From sloth, worldliness, and love of money;
from hardness of heart
and contempt for your word and your laws,
Good Lord, deliver us.

From sins of body and mind;
From the deceits of the world, the flesh,
    and the devil,
Good Lord, deliver us.

In all times of sorrow;
in all times of joy;
in the hour of death,
and at the day of judgement,
Good Lord, deliver us.

By the mystery of your holy incarnation;
by your birth, childhood, and obedience;
by your baptism, fasting, and temptation,
Good Lord, deliver us.

By your ministry in word and work;
by your mighty acts of power;
and by your preaching of the kingdom,
Good Lord, deliver us.

By your agony and trial;
by your cross and passion;
and by your precious death and burial,
Good Lord, deliver us.

By your mighty resurrection;
by your glorious ascension;
and by your sending of the Holy Spirit,
Good Lord, deliver us.

Give us true repentance;
forgive us our sins of negligence and ignorance
and our deliberate sins;
and grant us the grace of your Holy Spirit
to amend our lives according to your holy word.
Holy God,
holy and strong,
holy and immortal,
have mercy upon us.

or the words at section 45 may be used.

▶ 15   SILENCE is kept for a time, after which is said

President   Make our hearts clean, O God;
All   **and renew a right spirit within us.**

▶ 16   **All**   **Father eternal, giver of light and grace,**
we have sinned against you and against our
    neighbour,
in what we have thought,
in what we have said and done,
through ignorance, through weakness,
through our own deliberate fault.
We have wounded your love,

25

and marred your image in us.
We are sorry and ashamed,
and repent of all our sins.
For the sake of your Son Jesus Christ, who
died for us,
forgive us all that is past;
and lead us out from darkness
to walk as children of light.   Amen.

THE IMPOSITION OF ASHES

17   If the Imposition of Ashes is to follow, the president says

As a sign of the spirit of penitence with which we
shall keep this season of preparation for Easter, I
invite you to receive on your head in ash the sign
of the cross, the symbol of our salvation.

God our Father,
you create us from the dust of the earth:
grant that these ashes may be for us
a sign of our penitence
and a symbol of our mortality;
for it is by your grace alone
that we receive eternal life
in Jesus Christ our Saviour.   **Amen.**

18   The president and people receive the imposition of ashes, the
president first receiving the imposition from another
minister. At the imposition the minister says to each person

Remember that you are dust, and to dust you
shall return.
Turn away from sin and be faithful to Christ.

or he may impose ashes without use of words.

During the imposition silence may be kept, or A HYMN,
ANTHEM, or PSALM may be sung (see Lectionary p. 294).

19 One of these two prayers may be said by the president.

20   God our Father,
                the strength of all who put their trust in you,
                mercifully accept our prayers;
                and because, in our weakness,
                we can do nothing good without you,
                grant us the help of your grace,
                that in keeping your commandments
                we may please you, both in will and deed;
                through Jesus Christ our Lord. **Amen.**

    or

21   Almighty God,
                who forgives all who truly repent,
                have mercy upon *us*,
                pardon and deliver *us* from all *our* sins,
                confirm and strengthen *us* in all goodness
                and keep *us* in life eternal;
                through Jesus Christ our Lord. **Amen.**

22 If the Holy Communion is not to follow, section 46, Form A may be used here, after which the service concludes with THE LORD'S PRAYER, the prayer at section 40, and THE DISMISSAL (sections 42–44).

23 If the Holy Communion is to follow, any of the forms in section 46 may be used, and the service continues with THE PEACE.

THE PEACE

▶ 24 **Stand**

President   Being justified by faith, we have peace with God
                through our Lord Jesus Christ.
            The peace of the Lord be always with you
All   **and also with you.**

25 The president may say

> Let us offer one another a sign of peace.

and all may exchange a sign of peace.

THE PREPARATION OF THE GIFTS

► 26 The bread and wine are placed on the holy table.

27 The president may praise God for his gifts in appropriate words to which all respond

Blessed be God for ever.

28 The offerings of the people may be collected and presented. These words may be used.

> **Yours, Lord, is the greatness, the power,**
> **the glory, the splendour, and the majesty;**
> **for everything in heaven and on earth**
>   **is yours.**
> **All things come from you,**
> **and of your own do we give you.**

29 At the preparation of the gifts A HYMN may be sung.

THE EUCHARISTIC PRAYER

THE TAKING OF THE BREAD AND CUP AND THE GIVING OF THANKS

► 30 The president takes the bread and cup into his hands and replaces them on the holy table.

► 31 The president uses one of the four EUCHARISTIC PRAYERS (pp. 101–113) with this PROPER PREFACE.

> And now we give you thanks because through him you have given us the spirit of discipline, that we may triumph over evil and grow in grace.

THE COMMUNION

THE BREAKING OF THE BREAD AND
THE GIVING OF THE BREAD AND CUP

▶ 32 THE LORD'S PRAYER is said either as follows or in its
traditional form.

President   As our Saviour taught us, so we pray.
All

**Our Father in heaven,
hallowed be your name,
your kingdom come,
your will be done,
on earth as in heaven.
Give us today our daily bread.
Forgive us our sins
as we forgive those who sin against us.
Lead us not into temptation
but deliver us from evil.**

**For the kingdom, the power, and the glory
are yours
now and for ever.   Amen.**

▶ 33 The president breaks the consecrated bread, saying

We break this bread
to share in the body of Christ.
All   **Though we are many, we are one body,
because we all share in one bread.**

34 Either here or during the distribution one of the following
ANTHEMS may be said.

Lamb of God, you take away the sins of
the world:
have mercy on us.

Lamb of God, you take away the sins of
the world:
have mercy on us.

**Lamb of God, you take away the sins of
the world:
grant us peace.**

or **Jesus, Lamb of God: have mercy on us.
Jesus, bearer of our sins: have mercy on us.
Jesus, redeemer of the world: give us
your peace.**

▶ 35 Before the distribution the president says

Draw near with faith. Receive the body of our
Lord Jesus Christ which he gave for you, and his
blood which he shed for you.

Eat and drink in remembrance that he died for
you, and feed on him in your hearts by faith with
thanksgiving.

Jesus is the Lamb of God
who takes away the sins of the world.
Happy are those who are called to his supper.

All **Lord, I am not worthy to receive you,
but only say the word, and I shall be healed.**

▶ 36 The president and people receive the Communion. Any
authorized words of distribution may be used (see p. 7).
During the distribution HYMNS and ANTHEMS may be
sung. The Alternative Service Book provision is followed
for consecration of additional bread and wine and for
disposing of what remains.

AFTER COMMUNION

37 The president may say

Blessed is the man who meditates day and night
on the law of the Lord: he will yield fruit in due
season. *Psalm 1.3*

38 Silence may be kept and A HYMN may be sung.

▶ 39   Either or both of the following prayers is said.

40   President   Lord our God,
                grant us grace to desire you with our
                    whole heart;
                that so desiring, we may seek and find you;
                and so finding, may love you;
                and so loving, may hate those sins
                from which you have delivered us;
                through Jesus Christ our Lord.   **Amen.**

41   **All**   **Almighty God,**
                we thank you for feeding us
                with the body and blood of your Son
                  Jesus Christ.
                Through him we offer you our souls
                  and bodies
                to be a living sacrifice.
                Send us out
                in the power of your Spirit
                to live and work
                to your praise and glory.   **Amen.**

THE DISMISSAL

42   The president may say THIS BLESSING.

                Christ give you grace to grow in holiness, to
                deny yourselves, take up your cross, and follow
                him; and the blessing of God almighty, the
                Father, the Son, and the Holy Spirit, be among
                you, and remain with you always.   **Amen.**

▶ 43   President   Go in peace to love and serve the Lord.
          All   **In the name of Christ.**   **Amen.**

  or   President   Go in the peace of Christ.
          All   **Thanks be to God.**

▶ 44   The ministers and people depart.

APPENDICES

45 In place of the words at section 14 either of these forms may be used.

A

Minister   Our Lord Jesus Christ said, If you love me, keep my commandments; happy are those who hear the word of God and keep it. Hear then these commandments which God has given to his people, and take them to heart.

I am the Lord your God: you shall have no other gods but me.
You shall love the Lord your God with all your heart, with all your soul, with all your mind, and with all your strength.

All   **Amen. Lord, have mercy.**

Minister   You shall not make for yourself any idol.
God is spirit, and those who worship him must worship in spirit and in truth.

All   **Amen. Lord, have mercy.**

Minister   You shall not dishonour the name of the Lord your God.
You shall worship him with awe and reverence.

All   **Amen. Lord, have mercy.**

Minister   Remember the Lord's day and keep it holy.
Christ is risen from the dead: set your minds on things that are above, not on things that are on the earth.

All   **Amen. Lord, have mercy.**

Minister   Honour your father and mother.
Live as servants of God; honour one another; love the fellowship.

All   **Amen. Lord, have mercy.**

Minister	You shall not commit murder. Be reconciled to your neighbour; overcome evil with good.
All	**Amen. Lord, have mercy.**
Minister	You shall not commit adultery. Know that your body is a temple of the Holy Spirit.
All	**Amen. Lord, have mercy.**
Minister	You shall not steal. Be honest in all that you do and care for those in need.
All	**Amen. Lord, have mercy.**
Minister	You shall not be a false witness. Let everyone speak the truth.
All	**Amen. Lord, have mercy.**
Minister	You shall not covet anything which belongs to your neighbour. Remember the words of the Lord Jesus: It is more blessed to give than to receive. Love your neighbour as yourself, for love is the fulfilling of the law.
All	**Amen. Lord, have mercy.**

or **B**

Minister	God spoke all these words, saying, I am the Lord your God. You shall have no other gods before me.
	You shall not make for yourself a graven image.
	You shall not take the name of the Lord your God in vain.
	Remember the sabbath day, to keep it holy.
	Honour your father and your mother.
	You shall not kill.

You shall not commit adultery.

You shall not steal.

You shall not bear false witness against your neighbour.

You shall not covet anything that is your neighbour's.

Silence may be kept after each of these sentences.

46 Form A may be used at section 22. Any of these forms may be used at section 23.

A

Minister In the power of the Spirit and in union with Christ, let us pray to the Father.

Hear our prayers, O Lord our God.

All Hear us, good Lord.

Minister Govern and direct your holy Church; fill it with love and truth; and grant it that unity which is your will.

All Hear us, good Lord.

Minister Give us boldness to preach the gospel in all the world, and to make disciples of all the nations.

All Hear us, good Lord.

Minister Enlighten your ministers with knowledge and understanding, that by their teaching and their lives they may proclaim your word.

All Hear us, good Lord.

Minister Give your people grace to hear and receive your word, and to bring forth the fruit of the Spirit.

All Hear us, good Lord.

Minister Bring into the way of truth all who have erred and are deceived.

All Hear us, good Lord.

Minister	Strengthen those who stand; comfort and help the faint-hearted; raise up the fallen; and finally beat down Satan under our feet.
All	**Hear us, good Lord.**
Minister	Guide the leaders of the nations into the ways of peace and justice.
All	**Hear us, good Lord.**
Minister	Guard and strengthen your servant Elizabeth our Queen, that she may put her trust in you, and seek your honour and glory.
All	**Hear us, good Lord.**
Minister	Endue the High Court of Parliament and all the Ministers of the Crown with wisdom and understanding.
All	**Hear us, good Lord.**
Minister	Bless those who administer the law, that they may uphold justice, honesty, and truth.
All	**Hear us, good Lord.**
Minister	Give us the will to use the resources of the earth to your glory, and for the good of all.
All	**Hear us, good Lord.**
Minister	Bless and keep all your people.
All	**Hear us, good Lord.**
Minister	Help and comfort the lonely, the bereaved, and the oppressed.
All	**Lord, have mercy.**
Minister	Keep in safety those who travel, and all who are in danger.
All	**Lord, have mercy.**
Minister	Heal the sick in body and mind, and provide for the homeless, the hungry, and the destitute.
All	**Lord, have mercy.**

Minister	Show your pity on prisoners and refugees, and all who are in trouble.
All	**Lord, have mercy.**

Minister	Forgive our enemies, persecutors, and slanderers, and turn their hearts.
All	**Lord, have mercy.**

Minister	Hear us as we remember those who have died in the peace of Christ, both those who have confessed the faith and those whose faith is known to you alone, and grant us with them a share in your eternal kingdom.
All	**Lord, have mercy.**

Minister	Father, you hear those who pray in the name of your Son: grant that what we have asked in faith we may obtain according to your will; through Jesus Christ our Lord. **Amen.**

B

All	**Most merciful Lord,** **your love compels us to come in.** **Our hands were unclean,** **our hearts were unprepared;** **we were not fit** **even to eat the crumbs from under** ** your table.** **But you, Lord, are the God of our salvation,** **and share your bread with sinners.** **So cleanse and feed us** **with the precious body and blood of** ** your Son,** **that he may live in us and we in him;** **and that we, with the whole company** ** of Christ,** **may sit and eat in your kingdom. Amen.**

C

All   We do not presume
          to come to this your table, merciful Lord,
          trusting in our own righteousness,
          but in your manifold and great mercies.
          We are not worthy
          so much as to gather up the crumbs under
             your table.
          But you are the same Lord
          whose nature is always to have mercy.
          Grant us therefore, gracious Lord,
          so to eat the flesh of your dear Son
             Jesus Christ
          and to drink his blood,
          that we may evermore dwell in him
          and he in us.   Amen.

SERVICES OF PENITENCE

NOTES

1   **Occasions for Use**   These orders may be used on any day during Lent, or at other times of the year in preparation for a Sunday or other Holy Day. The Collect of the Day and other prayers of preparation for Holy Communion may be included in section 14.

2   **The Absolution**   When the service is led by a deacon or lay person, 'us' is said instead of 'you' in the Absolution (section 13).

3   **Silence**   Short periods of silence may be kept before or after the versicles and responses in section 10, and a longer period of silence is kept at section 11.

4   **The Holy Communion**   If it is desired to combine this service with the Holy Communion, it may end after section 13 or section 14 and the Holy Communion begins immediately at the Peace.

5   **Readings**   Other readings may be used.

SERVICES OF PENITENCE

ORDER A

1   At the entry of the ministers A HYMN, A CANTICLE, or A PSALM may be sung.

▶ 2   The minister welcomes the people.

> Grace, mercy, and peace from God our Father and the Lord Jesus Christ be with you all

All   **and also with you.**

3   The minister may say

> If we say we have no sin, we deceive ourselves, and the truth is not in us. If we confess our sins, God is faithful and just, and will forgive us our sins and cleanse us from all unrighteousness.
> *1 John 1.8,9*

> Compassion and forgiveness belong to the Lord our God, though we have rebelled against him.
> *Daniel 9.9*

> I will arise and go to my father, and I will say to him, 'Father, I have sinned against heaven and before you; I am no longer worthy to be called your son.' *Luke 15.18,19*

▶ 4   Minister   Almighty and everlasting God,
> you hate nothing that you have made
> and forgive the sins of all those who are penitent.
> Create and make in us new and contrite hearts,
> that, lamenting our sins
>   and acknowledging our wretchedness,

we may receive from you, the God of all mercy,
perfect forgiveness and peace;
through Jesus Christ our Lord.   **Amen.**

▶ 5   OLD TESTAMENT READING

Exodus 20.1-17 NEB

God spoke, and these were his words:

I am the Lord your God who brought you out of Egypt, out
of the land of slavery.

You shall have no other god to set against me.

You shall not make a carved image for yourself nor the
likeness of anything in the heavens above, or on the earth
below, or in the waters under the earth.

You shall not bow down to them or worship them; for I, the
Lord your God, am a jealous God. I punish the children for
the sins of the fathers to the third and fourth generations of
those who hate me. But I keep faith with thousands, with
those who love me and keep my commandments.

You shall not make wrong use of the name of the Lord your
God; the Lord will not leave unpunished the man who
misuses his name.

Remember to keep the sabbath day holy. You have six days
to labour and do all your work. But the seventh day is a
sabbath of the Lord your God; that day you shall not do any
work, you, your son or daughter, your slave or your slave-
girl, your cattle or the alien within your gates; for in six days
the Lord made heaven and earth, the sea, and all that is in
them, and on the seventh day he rested. Therefore the Lord
blessed the sabbath day and declared it holy.

Honour your father and your mother, that you may live
long in the land which the Lord your God is giving you.

You shall not commit murder.

You shall not commit adultery.

You shall not steal.

You shall not give false evidence against your neighbour.

You shall not covet your neighbour's house; you shall not covet your neighbour's wife, his slave, his slave-girl, his ox, his ass, or anything that belongs to him.

▶ 6   A CANTICLE OF REPENTANCE (*from The Prayer of Manasseh*)

This response may be used.

Lord, hear us: Lord, have mercy.

1 Lord almighty ⎮ God · of our ⎮ fathers:
    maker of highest heaven and the ⎮ mani · fold ⎮ order · of ⎮ earth;

2 All things are filled with awe and ⎮ tremble · at your ⎮ power:
    yet infinite and unsearchable ⎮ is your ⎮ merci · ful ⎮ promise. **R**

3 You are the Lord most high
    full of compassion ⎮ patience · and ⎮ mercy:
    you are moved when your children ⎮ suffer ⎮
    for their ⎮ sins.

4 In your goodness Lord you have promised ⌣
    forgiveness to those who ⎮ sin a ⎮ gainst you:
    in your boundless mercy you have appointed ⌣
    re ⎮ pentance · as the ⎮ way · to sal ⎮ vation. **R**

5 By reason of ⎮ my of ⎮ fences:
    I am not worthy to look up ⌣
    and be ⎮ hold the ⎮ heights of ⎮ heaven.

6 Now therefore do I bow the ⎮ knees · of my ⎮ heart:
    and ⎮ ask for ⎮ your for ⎮ giveness. **R**

7 I have sinned Lord | I have | sinned:
   I ack | nowledge | my trans | gression.

8 I humbly pray Spare me | Lord | spare me:
   do not be | angry | with me · for | ever. **R**

9 Deliver | me from | evil:
   do not a | bandon · me | to the | grave.

10 For you Lord are the | God · of the | penitent:
   in me you will | show forth | all your | goodness. **R**

11 Unworthy though I am
   you will save me | in your | mercy:
   and I will praise you continually |
   all the | days · of my | life.

12 For all the powers of heaven | sing your | praise:
   yours are the kingdom and the | glory |
   now · and for | ever. **R**

▶ 7 THE GOSPEL READING

Luke 18.9-14 NEB

Jesus told a parable, which was aimed at those who were sure
of their own goodness and looked down on everyone else.
'Two men went up to the temple to pray, one a Pharisee and
the other a tax gatherer. The Pharisee stood up and prayed
thus: "I thank thee, O God, that I am not like the rest of men,
greedy, dishonest, adulterous; or, for that matter, like this tax
gatherer. I fast twice a week; I pay tithes on all that I get."
But the other kept his distance and would not even raise his
eyes to heaven, but beat upon his breast, saying, "O God,
have mercy on me, sinner that I am." It was this man, I tell
you, and not the other, who went home acquitted of his sins.
For everyone who exalts himself will be humbled; and
whoever humbles himself will be exalted.'

▶ 8 THE SERMON

▶ 9   Minister   Let us hear our Lord's blessing on those who follow him, and let us confess our many failures to keep his way of life and truth.

▶ 10   **Kneel**

Minister   Our Lord Jesus Christ said, 'Blessed are the poor in spirit, for theirs is the kingdom of heaven.'
We have been proud and overbearing.
We have asserted our own importance and been jealous of others.
We have despised the weak and slandered those we envy and dislike.

Lord, have mercy.

All   **Christ, have mercy.**

Minister   Our Lord Jesus Christ said, 'Blessed are the meek, for they shall inherit the earth.'
We have been angry in our hearts and in our words.
We have returned evil for evil.
We have done violence ourselves and condoned the violence of others.

Lord, have mercy.

All   **Christ, have mercy.**

Minister   Our Lord Jesus Christ said, 'Blessed are those who weep, for they shall be consoled.'
We have not borne our own sorrow and suffering with the patience which comes from faith.
We have failed to show compassion and care for others who suffer.

Lord, have mercy.

All   **Christ, have mercy.**

Minister   Our Lord Jesus Christ said, 'Blessed are those who hunger and thirst after justice, for they shall be satisfied.'

We have cared little for the injustice, inequality,
and poverty around us.
We have hungered and thirsted for our own
comfort and safety,
and turned away from the injustice done to
others.

Lord, have mercy.

All   **Christ, have mercy.**

Minister   Our Lord Jesus Christ said, 'Blessed are the
merciful, for they shall obtain mercy.'
We have looked on our neighbour's faults and
weaknesses with a hard and intolerant eye.
We have failed to show understanding and
sympathy, but judged harshly and too soon.

Lord, have mercy.

All   **Christ, have mercy.**

Minister   Our Lord Jesus Christ said, 'Blessed are the pure
in heart, for they shall see God.'
We have been suspicious, distrustful, and
insincere in the thoughts of our hearts.
We have spoiled the joy and beauty of our senses
and our love through lust and self-indulgence.

Lord, have mercy.

All   **Christ, have mercy.**

Minister   Our Lord Jesus Christ said, 'Blessed are the
peacemakers, for they shall be called the children
of God.'
We have broken the loving peace of friends and
families with quarrelling and selfishness.
We have disturbed the peace of our land with
violence and civil strife.
We have filled the world with wars and the fear
of war.

Lord, have mercy.

All   **Christ, have mercy.**

Minister   Our Lord Jesus Christ said, 'Blessed are those
           who suffer persecution for the sake of justice,
           for theirs is the kingdom of heaven.'
           We have neglected in our prayers and in our
           charity those who are persecuted for their faith,
           their beliefs, or their race.
           We have encouraged or left unrebuked those
           who, in word or deed, deny the equality of the
           children of God.

           Lord, have mercy.
All   **Christ, have mercy.**

▶ 11   A period of silence is kept.

▶ 12   **All**   **Father eternal, giver of light and grace,**
              we have sinned against you and against our
                 neighbour,
              in what we have thought,
              in what we have said and done,
              through ignorance, through weakness,
              through our own deliberate fault.
              We have wounded your love,
              and marred your image in us.
              We are sorry and ashamed,
              and repent of our sins.
              For the sake of your Son Jesus Christ, who
                 died for us,
              forgive us all that is past;
              and lead us out from darkness
              to walk as children of light.   Amen.

▶ 13   Priest   Almighty God, our heavenly Father,
                who of his great mercy has promised forgiveness
                   of sins
                to all those who with heartfelt repentance and
                   true faith turn to him:

have mercy upon *you*,
pardon and deliver *you* from all *your* sins,
confirm and strengthen *you* in all goodness,
and bring *you* to the joy of heaven;
through Jesus Christ our Lord.   **Amen.**

14   A HYMN may be sung, and other suitable prayers may be
said.

▶ 15   **All**   **Our Father in heaven,**
hallowed be your name,
your kingdom come,
your will be done,
on earth as in heaven.
Give us today our daily bread.
Forgive us our sins
as we forgive those who sin against us.
Lead us not into temptation
but deliver us from evil.

For the kingdom, the power, and the glory
are yours
now and for ever.   Amen.

▶ 16   Minister   Lord our God,
grant us grace to desire you with our
whole heart;
that so desiring, we may seek and find you;
and so finding, may love you;
and so loving, may hate those sins
from which you have delivered us;
through Jesus Christ our Lord.   **Amen.**

▶ 17   Minister   Go in peace to love and serve the Lord.
All   **In the name of Christ.   Amen.**

▶ 18   The ministers and people depart.

46

ORDER B

1 At the entry of the ministers A HYMN, A CANTICLE, or A
   PSALM may be sung.

▶ 2 The minister welcomes the people.

Grace, mercy, and peace from God our Father
and the Lord Jesus Christ be with you all

All **and also with you.**

3 The minister may say

Hear the words of comfort our Saviour Christ
says to all who truly turn to him:
Come to me, all who labour and are heavy laden,
and I will give you rest. *Matthew 11.28*

God so loved the world that he gave his only
Son, that whoever believes in him should not
perish but have eternal life. *John 3.16*

Hear what Saint Paul says:
This saying is true and worthy of full acceptance,
that Christ Jesus came into the world to save
sinners. *1 Timothy 1.15*

Hear what Saint John says:
If anyone sins, we have an advocate with the
Father, Jesus Christ the righteous; and he is the
propitiation for our sins. *1 John 2.1*

▶ 4 Minister

Lord God our Father,
through our Saviour Jesus Christ
you have assured us of eternal life
and in baptism have made us one with him.
Deliver us from the death of sin
and raise us to new life in your love,
in the fellowship of the Holy Spirit,
by the grace of our Lord Jesus Christ. **Amen.**

▶ 5 OLD TESTAMENT READING

Hosea 6.1-6,11b; 7.1-2 NEB

Come, let us return to the Lord;
for he has torn us and will heal us,
he has struck us and he will bind up our wounds;
after two days he will revive us,
on the third day he will restore us,
that in his presence we may live.
Let us humble ourselves, let us strive to know the Lord,
whose justice dawns like morning light,
and its dawning is as sure as the sunrise.
It will come to us like a shower,
like spring rains that water the earth.

O Ephraim, how shall I deal with you?
How shall I deal with you, Judah?
Your loyalty to me is like the morning mist,
like dew that vanishes early.
Therefore have I lashed you through the prophets
and torn you to shreds with my words;
loyalty is my desire, not sacrifice,
not whole-offerings but the knowledge of God.

When I would reverse the fortunes of my people,
when I would heal Israel,
then the guilt of Ephraim stands revealed,
and all the wickedness of Samaria;
they have not kept faith.
They are thieves, they break into houses;
they are robbers, they strip people in the street,
little thinking that I have their wickedness ever in mind.
Now their misdeeds beset them
and stare me in the face.

► 6 *Psalm 103.1-12*

This response may be used.

The Lord is full of compassion and mercy.

1 Praise the Lord | O my | soul:
 and all that is within me | praise his | holy | name.

2 Praise the Lord | O my | soul:
 and for | get not | all his | benefits, **R**

3 Who forgives | all your | sin:
 and | heals | all · your in | firmities,

4 Who redeems your | life · from the | Pit:
 and crowns you with | mercy | and com | passion;

5 Who satisfies your being with | good | things:
 so that your | youth · is re | newed · like an |
  eagle's. **R**

6 The Lord | works | righteousness:
 and justice for | all who | are op | pressed.

7 He made known his | ways to | Moses:
 and his | works · to the | children · of | Israel. **R**

8 The Lord is full of com | passion · and | mercy:
 slow to anger | and of | great | goodness.

9 He will not | always · be | chiding:
 nor will he | keep his | anger · for | ever. **R**

10 He has not dealt with us ac | cording · to our | sins:
 nor rewarded us ac | cording | to our | wickedness.

11 For as the heavens are high a | bove the | earth:
 so great is his | mercy · over | those that | fear him;

12 As far as the east is | from the | west:
 so far has he | set our | sins | from us. **R**

49

► 7   THE GOSPEL READING

Luke 15.11-end RSV

Jesus said, 'There was a man who had two sons; and the younger of them said to his father, "Father, give me the share of property that falls to me." And he divided his living between them. Not many days later, the younger son gathered all he had and took his journey into a far country, and there he squandered his property in loose living. And when he had spent everything, a great famine arose in that country, and he began to be in want. So he went and joined himself to one of the citizens of that country, who sent him into his fields to feed swine. And he would gladly have fed on the pods that the swine ate; and no one gave him anything. But when he came to himself he said, "How many of my father's hired servants have bread enough and to spare, but I perish here with hunger! I will arise and go to my father, and I will say to him, 'Father, I have sinned against heaven and before you; I am no longer worthy to be called your son; treat me as one of your hired servants.' And he arose and came to his father. But while he was yet at a distance, his father saw him and had compassion, and ran and embraced him and kissed him. And the son said to him, "Father, I have sinned against heaven and before you; I am no longer worthy to be called your son." But the father said to his servants, "Bring quickly the best robe, and put it on him; and put a ring on his hand, and shoes on his feet; and bring the fatted calf and kill it, and let us eat and make merry; for this my son was dead, and is alive again; he was lost, and is found." And they began to make merry.

'Now his elder son was in the field; and as he came and drew near to the house, he heard music and dancing. And he called one of the servants and asked what this meant. And he said to him, "Your brother has come, and your father has killed the fatted calf, because he has received him safe and sound." But he was angry and refused to go in. His father came out and entreated him, but he answered his father, "Lo, these many years I have served you, and I never disobeyed your command; yet you never gave me a kid, that I might make merry with my friends. But when this son of yours came, who has devoured your living with harlots, you killed for him the fatted calf!" And he said to him, "Son, you are always with me and all that is mine is yours. It was fitting to make merry and be glad, for this your brother was dead, and is alive; he was lost, and is found.""

▶ 8   THE SERMON

▶ 9   Minister   God the Father looks for the return of his children who have strayed, and lovingly embraces them when they come back to him. Let us then with confidence draw near to the throne of grace, that we may receive mercy and find grace to help in time of need.

▶ 10   **Kneel**

Minister   Lord Jesus Christ, the Spirit of the Lord was upon you, because he anointed you to preach good news to the poor. He sent you to proclaim release to the captives and recovery of sight to the blind, to set at liberty those who were oppressed.

               Lord Jesus Christ, Son of God,

All   **have mercy on me, a sinner.**

Minister   Lord Jesus Christ, you ate and drank with sinners. For those who are well have no need of a physician, but those who are sick. You did not come to call the righteous, but sinners to repentance.

               Lord Jesus Christ, Son of God,

All   **have mercy on me, a sinner.**

Minister   Lord Jesus Christ, you said to scribes and
           pharisees who brought to you a woman caught
           in adultery, 'Let him who is without sin be the
           first to throw a stone.' And when they had gone
           away, one by one, you looked at her and said,
           'Has no one condemned you? Neither do I
           condemn you; go, and do not sin again.'

           Lord Jesus Christ, Son of God,
All   **have mercy on me, a sinner.**

Minister   Lord Jesus Christ, you called Zacchaeus to hasten
           and come down from the sycamore tree that he
           might receive you into his home. He gave half his
           goods to the poor and restored fourfold to any he
           had defrauded. You brought the joy of salvation
           to his house that day. For the Son of Man came to
           seek and to save the lost.

           Lord Jesus Christ, Son of God,
All   **have mercy on me, a sinner.**

Minister   Lord Jesus Christ, you welcomed the sinful
           woman when she knelt before you in the house
           of Simon. She washed your feet with her tears,
           wiped them with the hair of her head, and
           anointed you with costly ointment. You forgave
           her sin and sent her on her way in peace. Her sins,
           which were many, were forgiven, for she loved
           much.

           Lord Jesus Christ, Son of God,
All   **have mercy on me, a sinner.**

Minister   Lord Jesus Christ, you were crucified between
           two thieves, one on your right and one on your
           left. One of them hurled insults at you but the
           other confessed his sin and asked you to
           remember him when you came into your
           kingdom. In the hour of your agony, you said to
           the penitent thief, 'Today you will be with me in
           paradise.'

           Lord Jesus Christ, Son of God,
All   **have mercy on me, a sinner.**

Minister   Lord Jesus Christ, in the glory of your risen life
           you restored Simon Peter who had disowned
           you in the time of trial. You committed to him
           the care of your flock and once again called him
           to follow you in the way of the cross.

           Lord Jesus Christ, Son of God,
All   **have mercy on me, a sinner.**

► 11   A period of silence is kept.

► 12   **All**   **Father eternal, giver of light and grace,**
               we have sinned against you and against our
               neighbour,
               in what we have thought,
               in what we have said and done,
               through ignorance, through weakness,
               through our own deliberate fault.
               We have wounded your love,
               and marred your image in us.
               We are sorry and ashamed,
               and repent of all our sins.
               For the sake of your Son Jesus Christ, who
               died for us,
               forgive us all that is past;
               and lead us out from darkness
               to walk as children of light.   Amen.

▶ 13 Priest   Almighty God, our heavenly Father,
                  who of his great mercy has promised forgiveness
                      of sins
                  to all those who with heartfelt repentance and
                      true faith turn to him:
                  have mercy upon *you*.
                  pardon and deliver *you* from all *your* sins,
                  confirm and strengthen *you* in all goodness,
                  and bring *you* to the joy of heaven;
                  through Jesus Christ our Lord.   **Amen.**

14 A HYMN may be sung, and other suitable prayers may be
    said.

▶ 15 **All**   **Our Father in heaven,**
                  hallowed be your name,
                  your kingdom come,
                  your will be done,
                  on earth as in heaven.
                  Give us today our daily bread.
                  Forgive us our sins
                  as we forgive those who sin against us.
                  Lead us not into temptation
                  but deliver us from evil.

                  For the kingdom, the power, and the glory
                      are yours
                  now and for ever.   Amen.

► 16   Minister   Almighty God,
in whom we live and move and have our being,
you have made us for yourself
and our hearts are restless until they rest in you:
grant us purity of heart and strength of purpose,
that no selfish passion may hinder us from
   knowing your will,
no weakness from doing it;
but that in your light we may see light,
and in your service find our perfect freedom;
through Jesus Christ our Lord.   **Amen.**

► 17   Minister   Go in peace to love and serve the Lord.
   All   **In the name of Christ.   Amen.**

► 18   The ministers and people depart.

C

A FORM OF ABSOLUTION

which may be used for the quieting of the individual conscience.

God, the Father of all mercies,
through his Son Jesus Christ
forgives all who truly repent and believe in him:
by the ministry of reconciliation
which Christ has committed to his Church,
and in the power of the Spirit,
I declare that you are absolved from your sins,
in the name of the Father, and of the Son,
and of the Holy Spirit.

MORNING AND EVENING PRAYER IN LENT

The character of the season requires a choice of canticles which looks for austerity and penitence. Venite is the most suitable call to worship. If Benedictus and Magnificat are always said, the other canticles might well be Saviour of the World, the full form of A Song of Creation, and Te Deum vv 14–end (morning), together with The Song of Christ's Glory and Glory and Honour (evening). The shorter service would reflect a similar spirit of restraint.

NIGHT PRAYER

A SERVICE FOR LATE EVENING

This service, freely based on the ancient office of Compline, has been included here as of particular use for many occasions in Lent. It can be used to accompany Lenten addresses and meditations, or without an address as a late service with which to close the day. It is also appropriate in less formal settings as a conclusion to an evening of Bible study and prayer and is easily adapted for other parts of the Christian year.

This is above all a service of quietness and reflection before rest and is most effective when the ending is indeed an ending, without additions, conversation, or noise. If the service is in church, the lights are extinguished and those present depart in silence. If it is in the home they go quietly to bed.

NOTES

1   **Address**   If there is any address, instruction, meditation, or reading, it should precede this order.

2   **The Season**   This may be marked by the choice of hymn at section 6, an appropriate lesson at section 8, and the addition of a seasonal collect at section 15. For appropriate psalms and readings in Lent and Eastertide see the Lectionary. From Easter Day to Pentecost, 'Alleluia' may be added at sections 9 and 11.

NIGHT PRAYER

▶ 1   Minister   The Lord almighty grant us a quiet night, and a
                        perfect end.

        All   **Amen.**

  2   *The minister may say one or more of the following.*

> Lord, you are in the midst of us, and we are called
> by your name. Do not forsake us, O Lord our
> God. *Jeremiah 14.9*

> 'Come to me, all who labour and are heavy
> laden, and I will give you rest. Take my yoke
> upon you, and learn from me; for I am gentle and
> lowly in heart, and you will find rest for your
> souls. For my yoke is easy, and my burden is
> light.' *Matthew 11.28-end*

> Be sober, be watchful. Your adversary the devil
> prowls around like a roaring lion, seeking
> someone to devour. Resist him, firm in your
> faith. *1 Peter 5.8,9*

▶ 3   Minister   Let us reflect in silence on the day which is
                        ending, recalling our failures to love God and our
                        neighbour.

Silence is kept.

Let us confess our sins to almighty God.

▶ 4 **All**   **Almighty God, our heavenly Father,**
              we have sinned against you,
              through our own fault,
              in thought and word and deed,
              and in what we have left undone.
              For your Son our Lord Jesus Christ's sake,
              forgive us all that is past;
              and grant that we may serve you in newness
                of life
              to the glory of your name.   Amen.

▶ 5 Minister The almighty and most merciful God
              grant us pardon, absolution, and remission of all
                our sins,
              time for true repentance,
              amendment of life,
              and the grace and comfort of the Holy Spirit.
              Amen.

▶ 6 THIS HYMN, or another suitable hymn, is sung.

              To you before the end of day,
              creator of the world, we pray:
              in love unfailing hear our prayer,
              enfold us in your watchful care.

              Keep all disturbing dreams away,
              and hold the evil foe at bay.
              Repose untroubled let us find
              for soul and body, heart and mind.

              Almighty Father, this accord
              through Jesus Christ, your Son, our Lord:
              who reigns with you eternally
              in your blest Spirit's unity.

▶ 7 One or more PSALMS are said.
If no special psalms are appointed, the following are suitable.
Each psalm or group of psalms ends with

> **Glory to the Father and ' to the ' Son:**
> **and ' to the ' Holy ' Spirit;**
> **as it was in the be'ginning is ' now:**
> **and shall be for ' ever. ' A'men.**

Psalm 4

1 Answer me when I call O ' God of · my ' righteousness:
   when I was hard-pressed you set me free
      be gracious to me ' now and ' hear my ' prayer.

2 Sons of men   how long will you turn my ' glory ·
      to my ' shame:
   how long will you love what is worthless
      and ' seek ' after ' lies?

3 Know that the Lord has shown me his ' wonder·ful '
      kindness:
   when I call to the ' Lord ' he will ' hear me.

4 Tremble and ' do no ' sin:
   commune with your own heart up'on your '
      bed · and be ' still.

5 Offer the sacrifices ' that are ' right:
   and ' put your ' trust · in the ' Lord.

6 There are many who say   'Who will ' show us ·
      any ' good?
   the light of your countenance O ' Lord has ' gone '
      from us.'

7 Yet you have given my ' heart more ' gladness:
   than they have when their corn ' wine and '
      oil in'crease.

8 In peace I will lie ' down and ' sleep:
   for you alone Lord ' make me ' dwell in ' safety.

Psalm 16.7-end

7 I will bless the Lord who has | given · me | counsel:
   at night also | he · has in | structed · my | heart.

8 I have set the Lord | always · be | fore me:
   he is at my right | hand · and I | shall not | fail.

9 Therefore my heart is glad and my | spirit · re | joices:
   my flesh | also · shall | rest se | cure.

10 For you will not give me over to the | power of | death:
   nor suffer your | faithful one · to | see the | Pit.

11 You will show me the | path of | life:
   in your presence is the fullness of joy ★ and from
      your right hand flow de | lights for | ever | more.

Psalm 17.1-8

1 Hear my just cause O Lord give | heed to · my | cry:
   listen to my prayer that | comes from · no | lying | lips.

2 Let judgement for me come | forth from · your | presence:
   and let your | eyes dis | cern the | right.

3 Though you search my heart   and visit me |
      in the | night-time:
   though you try me by fire   you will | find no |
      wicked · ness | in me.

4 My mouth does not transgress like the | mouth of | others:
   for I have | kept the | word of · your | lips.

5 My steps have held firm in the way of |
      your com | mands:
   and my feet have not | stumbled | from your | paths.

6 I call upon you O God for you will | surely | answer:
   incline your ear to | me and | hear my | words.

7 Show me the wonders of your steadfast love
    O saviour of those who come to ǀ you for ǀ refuge:
  who by your right hand deliver them ⌣
    from ǀ those that · rise ǀ up a ǀ gainst them.

8 Keep me as the ǀ apple · of your ǀ eye:
  hide me under the ǀ shadow ǀ of your ǀ wings.

Psalm 31.1-5

1 To you Lord have I ǀ come for ǀ shelter:
  let me ǀ never · be ǀ put to ǀ shame.

2 O deliver me ǀ in your ǀ righteousness:
  incline your ear to me ǀ and be ǀ swift to ǀ save me.

3 Be for me a rock of refuge   a fortress ǀ to de ǀ fend me:
  for you are my ǀ high rock ǀ and my ǀ stronghold.

4 Lead me and guide me for your ǀ name's ǀ sake:
  bring me out of the net that they have secretly ⌣
    laid for me ★ for ǀ you ǀ are my ǀ strength.

5 Into your hands I com ǀ mit my ǀ spirit:
  you will redeem me ǀ O Lord ǀ God of ǀ truth.

Psalm 91

1 He who dwells in the shelter of the ǀ Most ǀ High:
  who abides under the ǀ shadow ǀ of the · Al ǀ mighty,

2 He will say to the Lord
    'You are my refuge ǀ and my ǀ stronghold:
  my ǀ God in ǀ whom I ǀ trust.'

3 For he will deliver you from the ǀ snare · of the ǀ hunter:
  and ǀ from the · de ǀ stroying ǀ curse.

4 He will cover you with his wings
    and you will be safe ǀ under · his ǀ feathers:
  his faithfulness will ǀ be your ǀ shield · and de ǀ fence.

5 You shall not be afraid of any ǀ terror · by ǀ night:
    or of the ǀ arrow · that ǀ flies by ǀ day,

6 Of the pestilence that walks a ǀ bout in ǀ darkness:
    or the ǀ plague · that de ǀ stroys at ǀ noonday.

7 A thousand may fall beside you
    and ten thousand at your ǀ right ǀ hand:
    but ǀ you it ǀ shall not ǀ touch;

8 Your own ǀ eyes shall ǀ see:
    and look on the re ǀ ward ǀ of the · un ǀ godly.

9 The Lord him ǀ self · is your ǀ refuge:
    you have ǀ made the · Most ǀ High your ǀ stronghold.

10 Therefore no ǀ harm · will be ǀ fall you:
    nor will any ǀ scourge come ǀ near your ǀ tent.

11 For he will com ǀ mand his ǀ angels:
    to ǀ keep you · in ǀ all your ǀ ways.

12 They will bear you ǀ up · in their ǀ hands:
    lest you dash your ǀ foot a ǀ gainst a ǀ stone.

13 You will tread on the ǀ lion · and the ǀ adder:
    the young lion and the serpent
    you will ǀ trample ǀ under ǀ foot.

14 'He has set his love upon me
    and therefore I ǀ will de ǀ liver him:
    I will lift him out of danger be ǀ cause · he has ǀ
    known my ǀ name.

15 'When he calls upon me ǀ I will ǀ answer him:
    I will be with him in trouble
    I will ǀ rescue him · and ǀ bring him · to ǀ honour.

16 'With long ǀ life · I will ǀ satisfy him:
    and ǀ fill him · with ǀ my sal ǀ vation.'

Psalm 134

1 Come bless the Lord   all you ˈservants · of the ˈ Lord:
    you that by night ˈ stand · in the ˈ house of · our ˈ God.

2 Lift up your hands toward the holy place ⌣
        and ˈ bless the ˈ Lord:
    may the Lord bless you from Zion
        the ˈ Lord who · made ˈ heaven · and ˈ earth.

Psalm 139.1-11,17-18

1 O Lord you have searched me ˈ out and ˈ known me:
    you know when I sit or when I stand
        you comprehend my ˈ thoughts ˈ long be ˈfore.

2 You discern my path   and the places ˈ where I ˈ rest:
    you are ac ˈquainted · with ˈ all my ˈ ways.

3 For there is not a ˈ word · on my ˈ tongue:
    but you Lord ˈ know it ˈ alto ˈgether.

4 You have encompassed me be ˈhind · and be ˈfore:
    and have ˈ laid your ˈ hand up ˈon me.

5 Such knowledge is too ˈ wonder·ful ˈ for me:
    so ˈ high · that I ˈcannot · en ˈdure it.

6 Where shall I ˈ go · from your ˈ spirit:
    or where shall I ˈ flee ˈ from your ˈ presence?

7 If I ascend into heaven ˈ you are ˈ there:
    if I make my bed in the grave ˈ you are ˈ there ˈ also.

8 If I spread out my wings to ˈwards the ˈ morning:
    or dwell in the ˈ utter·most ˈ parts · of the ˈ sea,

9 Even there your ˈ hand shall ˈ lead me:
    and ˈ your right ˈ hand shall ˈ hold me.

10 If I say   'Surely the ˈ darkness · will ˈ cover me:
    and the ˈ night ˈ will en ˈclose me',

11 The darkness is no darkness with you
   but the night is as | clear · as the | day:
   the darkness and the | light are | both a | like.

17 How deep are your thoughts to | me O | God:
   and how | great | is the | sum of them!

18 Were I to count them
   they are more in number | than the | sand:
   were I to come to the | end · I would | still be |
   with you.

▶ 8   THE READING FROM SCRIPTURE
      The following passages are suitable.

          Isaiah 26.3-5,7-9
          Isaiah 35.8-10
          Jeremiah 31.33-34
          Habakkuk 3.17-19
          John 3.19-21
          1 Corinthians 1.26-31
          1 Corinthians 2.10b-13
          Philippians 4.6-9

For Lent, Holy Week, and Easter see the Lectionary.

At the end the reader may say

          This is the word of the Lord.
All   **Thanks be to God.**

▶ 9   **All**   **Preserve us, O Lord, while waking,**
                 and guard us while sleeping,
              that awake we may watch with Christ,
              and asleep we may rest in peace.

From Easter Day to Pentecost **Alleluia!** may be added.

▶ 10 NUNC DIMITTIS is said or sung.

      1 Lord now you let your servant | go in | peace:
        your | word has | been ful | filled.

2 My own eyes have ˈ seen the · salˈ vation:
    which you have prepared in the ˈ sight of ˈ
        every ˈ people;

3 A light to re ˈ veal you · to the ˈ nations:
    and the ˈ glory · of your ˈ people ˈ Israel.

Glory to the Father and ˈ to the ˈ Son:
    and ˈ to the ˈ Holy ˈ Spirit;
as it was in the be ˈ ginning is ˈ now:
    and shall be for ˈ ever. ˈ A ˈ men.

► 11 **All**   **Preserve us, O Lord, while waking,**
                and guard us while sleeping,
                that awake we may watch with Christ,
                and asleep we may rest in peace.

From Easter Day to Pentecost **Alleluia!** may be added.

PRAYERS

► 12   Lord, have mercy on us,
        Christ, have mercy on us.
        Lord, have mercy on us.

► 13   **Our Father in heaven,**
        hallowed be your name,
        your kingdom come,
        your will be done,
        on earth as in heaven.
        Give us today our daily bread.
        Forgive us our sins
        as we forgive those who sin against us.
        Lead us not into temptation
        but deliver us from evil.

        For the kingdom, the power, and the glory
            are yours
        now and for ever.   Amen.

14   THESE VERSICLES AND RESPONSES may be said.

> Minister We will lie down in peace, and take our rest;
> **All** **for you alone, Lord, make us dwell in
> safety.**

> Minister Into your hands, O Lord, I commit my spirit;
> **All** **you will redeem me, O Lord God of truth.**

> Minister Keep us tonight, Lord, from all sin;
> **All** **have mercy on us, Lord, have mercy.**

> Minister Lord, hear our prayer;
> **All** **and let our cry come to you.**

15   One or more of these COLLECTS may be said.

> Visit, Lord, we pray, this place,
> and drive far from it all the snares of evil.
> Let your holy angels dwell here to keep us
> in peace,
> and may your blessing be upon us evermore;
> through Jesus Christ our Lord. **Amen.**

> Lighten our darkness, Lord, we pray;
> and in your mercy defend us
> from all perils and dangers of this night;
> for the love of your only Son,
> our Saviour Jesus Christ. **Amen.**

> Be with us, merciful God,
> and protect us through the silent hours of
> this night,
> so that we, who are wearied
> by the changes and chances of this fleeting world,
> may rest upon your eternal changelessness;
> through Jesus Christ our Lord. **Amen.**

> Look down, Lord, from your heavenly throne;
> lighten the darkness of the night
> with your celestial brightness;
> and from the children of light

banish the deeds of darkness;
through Jesus Christ our Lord.   **Amen.**

Lord Jesus Christ,
Son of the living God,
who at this evening hour rested in the sepulchre,
and sanctified the grave
to be a bed of hope to your people:
make us so deeply sorry for our sins,
which were the cause of your passion,
that when our bodies lie in the dust,
our souls may live with you;
for with the Father and the Holy Spirit
you live and reign, now and for ever.   **Amen.**

THIS COLLECT is appropriate on Sundays and from Easter
Day to Pentecost.

O Lord,
who by triumphing over the power of darkness
prepared our place in the new Jerusalem:
grant that we, who have this day
    given thanks for your resurrection,
may praise you in the city where you are
    the light;
for there with the Father and the Holy Spirit
you live and reign, now and for ever.   **Amen.**

▶ 16   Minister   The Lord be with you
        All   **and also with you.**

  17   Minister   Let us bless the Lord.
        All   **Thanks be to God.**

From Easter Day to Pentecost **Alleluia! Alleluia!** may be
added after both the versicle and the response.

▶ 18   Minister   The almighty and merciful Lord,
                    Father, Son, and Holy Spirit,
                    bless us and keep us, this night and for evermore.
        All   **Amen.**

PALM SUNDAY AND HOLY WEEK

PALM SUNDAY AND HOLY WEEK

PALM SUNDAY

INTRODUCTION

On Palm Sunday the Church commemorates Christ's entry into Jerusalem to accomplish his saving work by dying and rising again. The liturgy of the day has two distinctive features, the procession and the reading of the Passion Gospel.

The procession is the first of the commemorative liturgical actions of Holy Week which remind us of the main events in the last week of Jesus' ministry. Palm or other branches are carried, although they are secondary to the procession itself. But the procession does not only remind us of what happened then. It is an act of praise to Christ the King who reigns and triumphs on the cross, and it expresses our own readiness to take up our cross and follow our crucified and risen Lord, as we go with him to the place of suffering and death.

The practice of giving palm crosses is a well established one with devotional value. However in the procession it is not as telling a symbol as the carrying of branches whether of palm or of other trees, perhaps brought by members of the congregation. In the text of this service 'palms' are taken to include both palm crosses and other branches of any sort. The precise text of section 4 may be adapted to take account of local custom. There is no provision in this order for distribution of the palms within the service, for this would place the emphasis at the wrong point.

The reading of the Passion Gospel takes us into the heart of Holy Week. Although the services of this week are shaped by the historical commemoration of the events of the last week in Jesus' earthly life, taken together they form an extended celebration of the victory he won over death. The solemn reading or singing of the narrative of the passion and death of Jesus Christ is an essential part of the liturgy of Palm Sunday. For this reason the full form of the Passion should be used whenever possible. Coming after the procession, it reminds us that the kingly power of Christ is the power of self-giving love alone.

Because the procession and Passion Gospel are in themselves an eloquent proclamation of the gospel, the sermon may be omitted. The Creed and the Prayers of Penitence have also been made optional, where circumstances require that the service should not be longer than necessary. The Intercession should always be used, preferably in the special form provided.

At services other than the principal eucharist the commemoration of the Lord's entry into Jerusalem may be made without the procession, using sections 1–5.

NOTES

1   **The Procession**   Whenever possible the congregation gathers in a place apart from the church to which the procession will go. When this is not possible, sections 1–6 take place inside the church at a convenient place, and the procession takes place inside or outside the church, all or some of the congregation taking part, as circumstances permit.

2   **Palms**   Palms or other branches may be used. The congregation may bring palms with them, or be given them as they arrive.

3   **The Collect** (section 8)   The Collect is said after the procession, when all are in their places. It may be introduced by the words 'Let us pray' and a brief bidding, after which silence should be kept.

4   **The Psalm and Readings**   Three readings and a gradual psalm (sections 9–13) are provided. Wherever possible the whole provision should be used but, where pastoral need requires, it may be shortened by (a) omitting either the Old Testament or the New Testament reading, (b) omitting the psalm, (c) using the alternatives provided for in note 5 to the Lectionary (p. 293).

5   **The Passion**   The Gospel of the Passion should always be read. It is announced 'The Passion of our Lord Jesus Christ according to *N*' and concluded 'This is the Passion of the Lord'. No responses are used. It may be read or sung by three or more people. Afterwards silence may be kept. Where appropriate the congregation may be invited to sit during the reading of part of the Passion.

6   **Prayers of Penitence**   The Prayers of Penitence are omitted if they are normally used at the beginning of the eucharist, and may be omitted if they are normally used after the intercession.

7   **Liturgical Colour**   The liturgical colour is red.

PALM SUNDAY

COMMEMORATION OF
THE LORD'S ENTRY INTO JERUSALEM

1   When all are ready one of these ANTHEMS may be said or sung.

> Hosanna to the Son of David, the King of Israel.
> Blessed is he who comes in the name of the Lord.
> Hosanna in the highest.

or

> **Hosanna to the Son of David.**
> **Blessed is he who comes in the name of**
>   **the Lord.**
> Behold your king comes to you, O Zion,
> meek and lowly, sitting upon an ass.
> Ride on in the cause of truth
> and for the sake of justice.
> Your throne is the throne of God, it endures
>   for ever;
> and the sceptre of your kingdom is a
>   righteous sceptre.
> You have loved righteousness and hated evil:
> therefore God, your God, has anointed you
> with the oil of gladness above your fellows.
> **Hosanna to the Son of David.**
> **Blessed is he who comes in the name of**
>   **the Lord.**

▶ 2   The president welcomes the people.

> The Lord be with you
> **All**   **and also with you.**

▶ 3   The president introduces the celebration using these or other appropriate words.

> Dear friends in Christ, during Lent we have been preparing by works of love and self-sacrifice for the celebration of our Lord's death and resurrection. Today we come together to begin this solemn celebration in union with the Church throughout the world. Christ enters his own city to complete his work as our Saviour, to suffer, to die, and to rise again. Let us go with him in faith and love, so that, united with him in his sufferings, we may share his risen life.

▶ 4   The people hold up their palms while this prayer is said.

President   God our Saviour, whose Son Jesus Christ entered Jerusalem as Messiah to suffer and to die, let these palms be for us signs of his victory; and grant that we who bear them in his name may ever hail him as our King, and follow him in the way that leads to eternal life; who lives and reigns with you and the Holy Spirit, now and for ever. **Amen.**

5   One of these GOSPELS may be read.
When it is announced

All   **Glory to Christ our Saviour.**

Matthew 21.1-11 NEB

Jesus and his disciples were nearing Jerusalem; and when they reached Bethphage at the Mount of Olives, Jesus sent two of them with these instructions: 'Go to the village opposite, where you will at once find a donkey tethered with her foal beside her; untie them, and bring them to me. If anyone speaks to you, say, "Our Master needs them"; and he will let you take them at once.' This was to fulfil the prophecy which says, 'Tell the daughter of Zion, "Here is your king, who comes to you in gentleness, riding on an ass, riding on the foal of a beast of burden."'

The disciples went and did as Jesus had directed, and brought the donkey and her foal; they laid their cloaks on them and Jesus mounted. Crowds of people carpeted the road with their cloaks, and some cut branches from the trees to spread in his path. Then the crowd that went ahead and the others that came behind raised the shout: 'Hosanna to the Son of David! Blessings on him who comes in the name of the Lord! Hosanna in the heavens!'

When he entered Jerusalem the whole city went wild with excitement. 'Who is this?' people asked, and the crowd replied, 'This is the prophet Jesus, from Nazareth in Galilee.'

or Mark 11.1-10 RSV

When they drew near to Jerusalem, to Bethphage and Bethany, at the Mount of Olives, he sent two of his disciples, and said to them, 'Go into the village opposite you, and immediately as you enter it you will find a colt tied, on which no one has ever sat; untie it and bring it. If anyone says to you, "Why are you doing this?" say, "The Lord has need of it and will send it back here immediately."' And they went away, and found a colt tied at the door out in the open street; and they untied it. And those who stood there said to them, 'What are you doing, untying the colt?' And they told them what Jesus had said; and they let them go. And they brought the colt to Jesus, and threw their garments on it; and he sat upon it. And many spread their garments on the road, and others spread leafy branches which they had cut from the fields. And those who went before and those who followed cried out, 'Hosanna! Blessed is he who comes in the name of the Lord! Blessed is the kingdom of our father David that is coming! Hosanna in the highest!'

or Luke 19.29-40 RSV

When Jesus drew near to Bethphage and Bethany, at the mount that is called Olivet, he sent two of the disciples, saying, 'Go into the village opposite, where on entering you will find a colt tied, on which no one has ever yet sat; untie it and bring it here. If anyone asks you, "Why are you untying it?" you shall say this, "The Lord has need of it."' So those who were sent away and found it as he had told them. And as they were untying the colt, its owners said to them, 'Why are you untying the colt?' And they said, 'The Lord has need of it.' And they brought it to Jesus, and throwing their garments on the colt they set Jesus upon it. And as he rode along, they spread their garments on the road. As he was now drawing near, at the descent of the Mount of Olives, the whole multitude of the disciples began to rejoice and praise God with a loud voice for all the mighty works that they had seen, saying, 'Blessed is the King who comes in the name of the Lord! Peace in heaven and glory in the highest!' And some of the Pharisees in the multitude said to him, 'Teacher, rebuke your disciples.' He answered, 'I tell you, if these were silent, the very stones would cry out.'

At the end the reader says

This is the Gospel of Christ.

All   **Praise to Christ our Lord.**

▶ 6 The president or another minister addresses the people in these or similar words.

Let us go forth, praising Jesus our Messiah.

▶ 7 During the procession all hold palms in their hands, and appropriate hymns, psalms, or anthems are sung.

▶ 8 After the procession the president says THE COLLECT.

Almighty and everlasting God,
who in your tender love towards mankind

sent your Son our Saviour Jesus Christ
to take upon him our flesh
and to suffer death upon the cross:
grant that we may follow the example
    of his patience and humility,
and also be made partakers of his resurrection;
through Jesus Christ your Son our Lord,
who is alive and reigns with you
    and the Holy Spirit,
one God, now and for ever.   **Amen.**

THE MINISTRY OF THE WORD

▶ 9   **Sit**
OLD TESTAMENT READING

Isaiah 50.4-9a NEB

The Lord God has given me
the tongue of a teacher
and skill to console the weary
with a word in the morning;
he sharpened my hearing
that I might listen like one who is taught.
The Lord God opened my ears
and I did not disobey or turn back in defiance.
I offered my back to the lash,
and let my beard be plucked from my chin,
I did not hide my face from spitting and insult;
but the Lord God stands by to help me;
therefore no insult can wound me.
I have set my face like flint,
for I know that I shall not be put to shame,
because one who will clear my name is at my side.
Who dare argue against me? Let us confront one another.
Who will dispute my cause? Let him come forward.
The Lord God will help me;
who then can prove me guilty?

At the end the reader may say

This is the word of the Lord.

All   **Thanks be to God.**

▶ 10   *Psalm 69.1-3,7-9,21-23*

This response may be used.

**Christ Jesus became obedient unto death,
even death on a cross.**

1 Save | me O | God:
      for the waters have come up | even | to my | throat.

2 I sink in the deep mire | where no | footing is:
      I have come into deep waters | and the |
          flood sweeps | over me.

3 I am weary with crying out   my | throat is | parched:
      my eyes fail with | watching · so |
          long · for my | God.   **R**

7 For your sake have I | suffered · re | proach:
      and | shame has | covered · my | face.

8 I have become a stranger | to my | brothers:
      an alien | to my · own | mother's | sons.

9 Zeal for your house has | eaten · me | up:
      and the taunts of those who taunt | you have |
          fallen · on | me.   **R**

21 Insults have | broken · my | heart:
      my shame and dis | grace are | past | healing.

22 I looked for someone to have pity on me
          but | there was | no man:
      for some to | comfort me · but | found | none.

23 They gave me | poison · for | food:
      and when I was thirsty they | gave me |
          vinegar · to | drink.   **R**

▶ 11   **Sit**
NEW TESTAMENT READING (EPISTLE)

Philippians 2.5-11 NEB

Let your bearing towards one another arise out of your life in
Christ Jesus. For the divine nature was his from the first; yet
he did not think to snatch at equality with God, but made
himself nothing, assuming the nature of a slave. Bearing the
human likeness, revealed in human shape, he humbled
himself, and in obedience accepted even death – death on a
cross. Therefore God raised him to the heights and bestowed
on him the name above all names, that at the name of Jesus
every knee should bow – in heaven, on earth, and in the
depths – and every tongue confess, 'Jesus Christ is Lord', to
the glory of God the Father.

At the end the reader may say

        This is the word of the Lord.

All   **Thanks be to God.**

12   A CANTICLE, A HYMN, or A PSALM may be used.

▶ 13   **Stand**
THE PASSION GOSPEL
(See pp. 118–136 and 143–168.)

At the end the reader says

        This is the Passion of the Lord.

No response is made.

14   A SERMON may be preached.

15   THE NICENE CREED may be said.

THE INTERCESSION

▶ 16 Minister   We stand with Christ in his suffering.

For forgiveness for the many times we have
denied Jesus, let us pray to the Lord.

All   **Lord, have mercy.**

Minister   For grace to seek out those habits of sin which
mean spiritual death, and by prayer and self-
discipline to overcome them, let us pray to the
Lord.

All   **Lord, have mercy.**

Minister   For Christian people, that through the suffering
of disunity there may grow a rich union in
Christ, let us pray to the Lord.

All   **Lord, have mercy.**

Minister   For those who make laws, interpret them, and
administer them, that our common life may be
ordered in justice and mercy, let us pray to the
Lord.

All   **Lord, have mercy.**

Minister   For those who still make Jerusalem a battle-
ground, let us pray to the Lord.

All   **Lord, have mercy.**

Minister   For those who have the courage and honesty to
work openly for justice and peace, let us pray to
the Lord.

All   **Lord, have mercy.**

Minister   For those in the darkness and agony of isolation,
that they may find support and encouragement,
let us pray to the Lord.

All   **Lord, have mercy.**

Minister For those who, weighed down with hardship,
failure, or sorrow, feel that God is far from them,
let us pray to the Lord.

All **Lord, have mercy.**

Minister For those who are tempted to give up the way of
the cross, let us pray to the Lord.

All **Lord, have mercy.**

Minister That we, with those who have died in faith, may
find mercy in the day of Christ, let us pray to the
Lord.

All **Lord, have mercy.**

17 THE TRISAGION may be said.

> **Holy God,**
> **holy and strong,**
> **holy and immortal,**
> **have mercy upon us.**

18 THE PRAYERS OF PENITENCE may be omitted.

THE MINISTRY OF THE SACRAMENT

THE PEACE

▶ 19 **Stand**

President Christ is our peace.
He has reconciled us to God
in one body by the cross.
We meet in his name and share his peace.

The peace of the Lord be always with you

All **and also with you.**

20 The president may say

Let us offer one another a sign of peace.

and all may exchange a sign of peace.

THE PREPARATION OF THE GIFTS

▶ 21   The bread and wine are placed on the holy table.

22   The president may praise God for his gifts in appropriate
words to which all respond

Blessed be God for ever.

23   The offerings of the people may be collected and presented.
These words may be used.

> **Yours, Lord, is the greatness, the power,**
> **the glory, the splendour, and the majesty;**
> **for everything in heaven and on earth**
>   **is yours.**
> **All things come from you,**
> **and of your own do we give you.**

24   At the preparation of the gifts A HYMN may be sung.

THE EUCHARISTIC PRAYER

THE TAKING OF THE BREAD AND CUP AND THE GIVING OF THANKS

▶ 25   The president takes the bread and cup into his hands and
replaces them on the holy table.

▶ 26   The president uses one of the four EUCHARISTIC PRAYERS
(pp. 101–113) with either of these PROPER PREFACES.

> And now we give you thanks because for our sins
> he was lifted high upon the cross that he might
> draw the whole world to himself; and, by his
> suffering and death, became the source of eternal
> salvation for all who put their trust in him.

or

> And now we give you thanks because for our
> salvation he was obedient even to death on the

cross. The tree of shame was made the tree of glory; and where life was lost, there life has been restored.

THE COMMUNION

THE BREAKING OF THE BREAD AND THE GIVING OF THE BREAD AND CUP

▶ 27   THE LORD'S PRAYER is said either as follows or in its traditional form.

▶ 28   President   As our Saviour taught us, so we pray.

All   **Our Father in heaven,**
hallowed be your name,
your kingdom come,
your will be done,
on earth as in heaven.
Give us today our daily bread.
Forgive us our sins
as we forgive those who sin against us.
Lead us not into temptation
but deliver us from evil.

For the kingdom, the power, and the glory
  are yours
now and for ever.   Amen.

▶ 29   The president breaks the consecrated bread, saying

We break this bread
to share in the body of Christ.

All   **Though we are many, we are one body,**
because we all share in one bread.

30 Either here or during the distribution one of the following
ANTHEMS may be said.

> Lamb of God, you take away the sins of
>   the world:
> have mercy on us.
>
> Lamb of God, you take away the sins of
>   the world:
> have mercy on us.
>
> Lamb of God, you take away the sins of
>   the world:
> grant us peace.

or Jesus, Lamb of God: have mercy on us.
Jesus, bearer of our sins: have mercy on us.
Jesus, redeemer of the world: give us
   your peace.

▶ 31 Before the distribution the president says

> Draw near with faith. Receive the body of our
> Lord Jesus Christ which he gave for you, and his
> blood which he shed for you.
>
> Eat and drink in remembrance that he died for
> you, and feed on him in your hearts by faith with
> thanksgiving.
>
> Jesus is the Lamb of God
> who takes away the sins of the world.
> Happy are those who are called to his supper.

All **Lord, I am not worthy to receive you,**
but only say the word, and I shall be healed.

▶ 32 The president and people receive the Communion. Any
authorized words of distribution may be used (see p. 7).
During the distribution HYMNS and ANTHEMS may be
sung. The Alternative Service Book provision is followed
for consecration of additional bread and wine and for
disposing of what remains.

AFTER COMMUNION

33　The president may say

> Jesus said, Father, if this cup may not pass from
> me, but I must drink it, your will be done.
> *Matthew 26.42*

34　Silence may be kept and A HYMN may be sung.

▶ 35　Either or both of the following prayers is said.

36　President　Almighty God,
whose most dear Son went not up to joy
　　but first he suffered pain,
and entered not into glory before he
　　was crucified:
mercifully grant that we, walking in the way of
　　the cross,
may find it none other than the way of life
　　and peace;
through Jesus Christ our Lord.　　**Amen.**

37　**All**　　　**Almighty God,**
we thank you for feeding us
with the body and blood of your Son
**　　Jesus Christ.**
Through him we offer you our souls
**　　and bodies**
to be a living sacrifice.
Send us out
in the power of your Spirit
to live and work
to your praise and glory.　　Amen.

THE DISMISSAL

38 The president may say THIS BLESSING.

Christ crucified draw you to himself, to find in him a sure ground for faith, a firm support for hope, and the assurance of sins forgiven; and the blessing of God almighty, the Father, the Son, and the Holy Spirit, be among you, and remain with you always. **Amen.**

▶ 39 President   Go in peace to love and serve the Lord.
    All   **In the name of Christ.   Amen.**

or

President   Go in the peace of Christ.
All   **Thanks be to God.**

▶ 40 The ministers and people depart.

MORNING AND EVENING PRAYER IN HOLY WEEK

From Sunday to Wednesday Venite is a suitable call to worship; if Benedictus and Magnificat are used each day, the second canticle might be Saviour of the World (morning) and Glory and Honour (evening).

The appropriate change of character is achieved if on the last three days the service begins abruptly at the psalm (omitting any call to worship and responses), omits all provision for 'Glory to the Father . . .', retains Benedictus and Magnificat, supported by Te Deum vv 14-end and The Song of Christ's Glory, and ends with the Lord's Prayer and the collects (omitting Creed and responses).

The solemnity of this week is emphasized by using the full order of psalms, readings, and canticles.

The form of intercession at section 16 on p. 83 may also appropriately be used at Morning and Evening Prayer and the Holy Communion in Holy Week.

PRAYERS ON THE PASSION

1   *Morning*   Like a lamb that is led to the slaughter, and like and sheep that before its shearer sits dumb, so he opened not his mouth.

It was the third hour;
and they crucified him.

Lord Jesus Christ, Son of the living God, at the third hour you were led out to the pain of the cross for the salvation of the world; by the virtue of your saving passion blot out our sins and bring us to the glory of your eternal joy, for you are alive and reign, God, now and for ever.

2   *Mid-Day*   When I am lifted up from the earth, I will draw all men to myself.

Jesus, remember me
when you come in your kingly power.

Most gracious Jesus, our Lord and our God, who at this hour bore our sins in your body on the tree that we might die to sin and live to righteousness, have mercy on us, now and at the hour of death; and grant us, with all your people who now recall your saving passion, a holy and peaceful life in this world, and, through your grace, eternal glory in the life to come, where, with the Father and the Holy Spirit, you are alive and reign, one God, now and for ever.

3 *Afternoon*   When he suffered, he did not threaten; but he trusted to him who judges justly.

Even here your hand shall lead me;
and your right hand shall hold me.

Hear us, merciful Jesus, and remember the hour in which you commended your spirit into the hands of your heavenly Father; by this your most precious death help us, that being dead to the world we may live to you alone; and that at the hour of leaving this mortal life we may be received into your eternal kingdom, there to reign with you for ever and ever.

Lord Jesus Christ, Son of the living God, who at the ninth hour with outstretched hands and bowed head commended your spirit to God the Father, and by your death unlocked the gates of paradise; grant that in the hour of our death we may come to know you, the true paradise, for ever and ever.

4   O God of all the nations of the earth, remember those who, though created in your image, are ignorant of your love; and, in fulfilment of the sacrifice of your Son Jesus Christ, let the prayers and labours of your Church deliver them from false faith and unbelief, and bring them to worship you; through him who is the resurrection and the life of all who put their trust in you, Jesus Christ our Lord.

5   Lord Jesus Christ, Son of the living God, set your passion, cross, and death between your judgement and us, now and at the hour of our death. Give mercy and grace to the living, rest to the faithful departed, to your holy Church peace and concord, and to us sinners eternal life and

glory; for you are alive and reign with the Father and the Holy Spirit, one God, now and for ever.

6   Lord Jesus, by the loneliness of your suffering on the cross, be near to all who are desolate and in pain and sorrow; and let your presence transform their sorrow into comfort, and their loneliness into fellowship with you; for the sake of your tender mercy.

7   Lord God our heavenly Father, regard, we pray, with your divine pity the pains of all your children; and grant that the passion of our Lord and his infinite love may make fruitful for good the tribulations of the innocent, the sufferings of the sick, and the sorrows of the bereaved; through him who suffered in our flesh and died for our sake, your Son our Saviour Jesus Christ.

8   Gracious Lord Jesus, who died on the cross for us; remember all who are sick and dying. May they neglect nothing which is necessary to making their peace with you before they die; save them from the snares of sin and evil; and bring them to a perfect end; for the sake of your loving mercy.

9   Blessed be your name, O Jesu, Son of the most high God; blessed be the sorrow you suffered when your holy hands and feet were nailed to the tree; and blessed your love when, the fullness of pain accomplished, you gave your soul into the hands of the Father; so by your cross and precious blood redeeming all the world, all longing souls departed and the numberless unborn; for you are now alive and reign in the glory of the eternal Trinity, God for ever and ever.

10   Thanks be to God, who gives us the victory
through our Lord Jesus Christ.

We praise you, Lord Jesus Christ, Son of God,
for you submitted to the discipline of a son's
obedience, and perfectly revealed in your death
the loving nature of the Father.

We praise you, Lord Jesus Christ, Son of Man,
for as champion of man and for his sake you
entered the battle against evil, and won the
complete victory over its power.

We praise you, Lord Jesus Christ, Servant of
God, for you accepted the suffering of those who
seek to be at one with those they serve, and by
your sacrifice made us one with God.

Thanks be to God who gives us the victory
through our Lord Jesus Christ.

11   Lord Jesus Christ, we thank you
for all the benefits you have won for us,
for all the pains and insults you have borne for us.
Most merciful redeemer,
friend and brother,
may we know you more clearly,
love you more dearly,
and follow you more nearly,
day by day.

12   Lord Jesus Christ,
Son of God,
have mercy on me,
a sinner.

13   Lord Jesus Christ, who, about to institute your
holy sacrament at the Last Supper, washed the
feet of the apostles, and taught us by your
example the grace of humility; cleanse us, we

pray, from all stain of sin, that we may be prepared to share your holy mysteries; for you are alive and reign with the Father and the Holy Spirit, one God, now and for ever.

14 God, our Judge and Saviour, set before us the vision of your purity, and let us see our sins in the light of your holiness. Pierce our self-contentment with the shafts of your burning love, and let that love consume all that hinders us from the perfect service of your kingdom; for as your holiness is our judgement, so are your wounds our salvation.

15 'My God, why have you forsaken me?'

Lord Jesus Christ, who for us endured the horror of deep darkness; teach us by the depth of your agony the vileness of our sin, and so bind us to yourself in bonds of gratitude and love, that we may be united with you in your perfect sacrifice, our Saviour, our Lord, and our God.

16 Soul of Christ, sanctify me,
Body of Christ, save me.
Blood of Christ, refresh me.
Water from the side of Christ, wash me.
Passion of Christ, strengthen me.
O good Jesus, hear me.
Within your wounds hide me.
Let me never be separated from you.
From the power of darkness defend me.
In the hour of my death, call me
  and bid me come to you,
that with your saints I may praise you
  for ever and ever.

17 *After Communion* Lord, we have celebrated the memorial of your Son's eternal sacrifice. By his passion guard and defend us; by his wounds heal us; by his blood wash us from sin; by his death bring us to everlasting glory; for in him is the fulfilment of our hopes and longings, now and for ever.

18 Lord God, whose Son is the true vine and the source of life, ever giving himself that the world might live; may we so receive within ourselves the power of his death and passion, that, in this cup of his life, we may share his glory and be made perfect in his love; for he is alive and reigns with you and the Holy Spirit, God, now and for ever.

19 We adore you, Christ, and we bless you;
because by your holy cross you have redeemed the world.

20 Saviour of the world, you have redeemed us by your passion and cross.
Save us and help us, we humbly pray.

21 *Ending* The glorious passion of our Lord Jesus Christ bring us to the joys of paradise.

THE AGAPE
WITH THE HOLY COMMUNION

Agape is strictly the New Testament word for love. It was also applied to a fellowship meal or love feast which, in the early Church, often occurred in association with the eucharist. This was common enough in the second to fourth centuries, as is shown by references in the writings of Ignatius and Tertullian. But it created problems of discipline and fell into disuse. The last reference is in a Council of 692.

Jesus enjoyed regular table fellowship with his disciples (Luke 13.26), and the sharing of a meal together has remained a sign of the intimate fellowship inseparable from true Christian discipleship. But the agape as a distinctive Christian celebration must retain its connection with the eucharist. It is this connection which provides the agape with any validity it may have in the modern age.

Its history, and not least the experience related in 1 Cor. 11.17-34, shows that, where it is introduced, there is need of a high degree of discipline. There should be careful preparation of the people, perhaps an indication of how conversation should be conducted, and meticulous attention to practical details. The service may take place in church, hall, or home, with the people seated at tables or moving around for a buffet-style meal. Everyone should be in visual contact with the place where the bread is to be broken and the sermon preached. If the bread and wine are to be passed round from hand to hand, there must be a clear and obvious route. There may be need to help the elderly. The food should be simple. There should be a minimum of noise and bustle.

Within the Rite A service there is scope for informality. The people should be relaxed, not necessarily standing to sing, or kneeling to pray. A sequence of hymns or songs might be sung.

There could be discussion instead of a sermon. Extempore prefaces might be appropriate, allowing for the expression of thanksgiving. But in all this the structure of the liturgy should stand out. It is necessary for the president to steer, order, and guide the congregation so that all is done without uncertainty and with dignity.

The agape might be combined with the Holy Communion at any time. It is appropriate on Monday, Tuesday, and Wednesday in Holy Week. Some may particularly wish to use it on the evening of Maundy Thursday.

The following order may be found suitable (the numbers are those of ASB Rite A) or the meal may follow the eucharist.

1   Sentence

2   Greeting

        The introductory part of the meal.

3–8   Prayers of Penitence

11   Collect

12–18 The Ministry of the Word

        The main course of a simple meal may be taken here.

20–21 The Intercession

30–31 The Peace

        The people may move about as they exchange the Peace.

        The second course may be taken here.

32–35 The Preparation of the Gifts

38–49 The Eucharistic Prayer and Communion

        The consecrated bread and wine may be passed reverently round the tables or the communicants may move to a central point.

50–56 After Communion

EUCHARISTIC PRAYERS
FROM HOLY COMMUNION RITE A

EUCHARISTIC PRAYERS
FROM HOLY COMMUNION RITE A

FIRST EUCHARISTIC PRAYER

President   The Lord be with you   or   The Lord is here.
All   **and also with you.**   **His Spirit is with us.**

President   Lift up your hearts.
All   **We lift them to the Lord.**

President   Let us give thanks to the Lord our God.
All   **It is right to give him thanks and praise.**

President   It is indeed right,
it is our duty and our joy,
at all times and in all places
to give you thanks and praise,
holy Father, heavenly King,
almighty and eternal God,
through Jesus Christ your only Son our Lord.

For he is your living Word;
through him you have created all things from
      the beginning,
and formed us in your own image.

Through him you have freed us from the
      slavery of sin,
giving him to be born as man and to die upon
      the cross;
you raised him from the dead
and exalted him to your right hand on high.

Through him you have sent upon us
your holy and life-giving Spirit,
and made us a people for your own possession.

[PROPER PREFACE]

Therefore with angels and archangels,
and with all the company of heaven,
we proclaim your great and glorious name,
for ever praising you and saying:

All   **Holy, holy, holy Lord,**
God of power and might,
heaven and earth are full of your glory.
Hosanna in the highest.

THIS ANTHEM may also be used.

Blessed is he who comes in the name of
the Lord.
Hosanna in the highest.

President   Accept our praises, heavenly Father,
through your Son our Saviour Jesus Christ;
and as we follow his example and obey
   his command,
grant that by the power of your Holy Spirit
these gifts of bread and wine
may be to us his body and his blood;

Who in the same night that he was betrayed,
took bread and gave you thanks;
he broke it and gave it to his disciples, saying,
Take, eat; this is my body which is given for you;
do this in remembrance of me.
In the same way, after supper
he took the cup and gave you thanks;
he gave it to them, saying,
Drink this, all of you;
this is my blood of the new covenant,
which is shed for you and for many for the
   forgiveness of sins.
Do this, as often as you drink it,
in remembrance of me.

All   *   **Christ has died:**
Christ is risen:
Christ will come again.

President   Therefore, heavenly Father,
we remember his offering of himself
made once for all upon the cross,
and proclaim his mighty resurrection and
     glorious ascension.
As we look for his coming in glory,
we celebrate with this bread and this cup
his one perfect sacrifice.

Accept through him, our great high priest,
this our sacrifice of thanks and praise;
and as we eat and drink these holy gifts
in the presence of your divine majesty,
renew us by your Spirit,
inspire us with your love,
and unite us in the body of your Son,
Jesus Christ our Lord.

---

* Alternative Acclamations

Dying you destroyed our death,
rising you restored our life.
Lord Jesus, come in glory.

When we eat this bread and drink this cup,
we proclaim your death, Lord Jesus,
until you come in glory.

Lord, by your cross and resurrection
you have set us free.
You are the Saviour of the world.

Through him, and with him, and in him,
by the power of the Holy Spirit,
with all who stand before you in earth
    and heaven,
we worship you, Father almighty,
in songs of everlasting praise:

All   **Blessing and honour and glory and power
be yours for ever and ever.   Amen.**

Silence may be kept.

SECOND EUCHARISTIC PRAYER

President   The Lord be with you or The Lord is here.
All   **and also with you.   His Spirit is with us.**

President   Lift up your hearts.
All   **We lift them to the Lord.**

President   Let us give thanks to the Lord our God.
All   **It is right to give him thanks and praise.**

President   It is indeed right,
it is our duty and our joy,
at all times and in all places
to give you thanks and praise,
holy Father, heavenly King,
almighty and eternal God,
through Jesus Christ your only Son our Lord.

The following may be omitted if a Proper Preface is used.

For he is your living Word;
through him you have created all things from
    the beginning,
and formed us in your own image.

Through him your have freed us from the
    slavery of sin,

giving him to be born as man and to die upon
   the cross;
you raised him from the dead
and exalted him to your right hand on high.

Through him you have sent upon us
your holy and life-giving Spirit,
and made us a people for your own possession.

[PROPER PREFACE]

Therefore with angels and archangels,
and with all the company of heaven,
we proclaim your great and glorious name,
for ever praising you and saying:

All **Holy, holy, holy Lord,**
God of power and might,
heaven and earth are full of your glory.
Hosanna in the highest.

THIS ANTHEM may also be used.

Blessed is he who comes in the name of
the Lord.
Hosanna in the highest.

President Hear us, heavenly Father,
through Jesus Christ your Son our Lord,
through him accept our sacrifice of praise;
and grant that by the power of your Holy Spirit
these gifts of bread and wine
may be to us his body and his blood;

Who in the same night that he was betrayed,
took bread and gave you thanks;
he broke it and gave it to his disciples, saying,
Take, eat; this is my body which is given for you;
do this in remembrance of me.

In the same way, after supper
he took the cup and gave you thanks;
he gave it to them, saying,
Drink this, all of you;
this is my blood of the new covenant,
which is shed for you and for many for the
    forgiveness of sins.
Do this, as often as you drink it,
in remembrance of me.

All ★ **Christ has died:**
Christ is risen:
Christ will come again.

President   Therefore, Lord and heavenly Father,
having in remembrance his death once for all
    upon the cross,
his resurrection from the dead,
and his ascension into heaven,
and looking for the coming of his kingdom,
we make with this bread and this cup
the memorial of Christ your Son our Lord.

Accept through him this offering of our duty
    and service;
and as we eat and drink these holy gifts

★ Alternative Acclamations

Dying you destroyed our death,
rising you restored our life.
Lord Jesus, come in glory.

When we eat this bread and drink this cup,
we proclaim your death, Lord Jesus,
until you come in glory.

Lord, by your cross and resurrection
you have set us free.
You are the Saviour of the world.

in the presence of your divine majesty,
fill us with your grace and heavenly blessing;
nourish us with the body and blood of your Son,
that we may grow into his likeness
and, made one by your Spirit,
become a living temple to your glory.

Through Jesus Christ our Lord,
by whom, and with whom, and in whom,
in the unity of the Holy Spirit,
all honour and glory be yours, almighty Father,
from all who stand before you in earth
   and heaven,
now and for ever.   **Amen.**

Silence may be kept.

THIRD EUCHARISTIC PRAYER

President	The Lord be with you or The Lord is here.
All	**and also with you.** **His Spirit is with us.**

President   Lift up your hearts.
All   **We lift them to the Lord.**

President   Let us give thanks to the Lord our God.
All   **It is right to give him thanks and praise.**

President   Father, we give you thanks and praise
through your beloved Son Jesus Christ,
your living Word through whom you have
   created all things;

Who was sent by you, in your great goodness,
   to be our Saviour;
by the power of the Holy Spirit he took flesh
and, as your Son, born of the blessed Virgin,
was seen on earth
and went about among us;

He opened wide his arms for us on the cross;

he put an end to death by dying for us
and revealed the resurrection by rising to
new life;
so he fulfilled your will and won for you a
holy people.

[PROPER PREFACE]

Therefore with angels and archangels,
and with all the company of heaven,
we proclaim your great and glorious name,
for ever praising you and saying:

All   **Holy, holy, holy Lord,**
God of power and might,
heaven and earth are full of your glory.
Hosanna in the highest.

THIS ANTHEM may also be used.

Blessed is he who comes in the name of
the Lord.
Hosanna in the highest.

President   Lord, you are holy indeed, the source of
all holiness;
grant that, by the power of your Holy Spirit,
and according to your holy will,
these your gifts of bread and wine
may be to us the body and blood of our Lord
Jesus Christ;

Who in the same night that he was betrayed,
took bread and gave you thanks;
he broke it and gave it to his disciples, saying,
Take, eat; this is my body which is given for you;
do this in remembrance of me.

In the same way, after supper
he took the cup and gave you thanks;
he gave it to them, saying,
Drink this, all of you;
this is my blood of the new covenant,
which is shed for you and for many for the
    forgiveness of sins.
Do this, as often as you drink it,
in remembrance of me.

All   ★   **Christ has died:**
Christ is risen:
Christ will come again.

President   And so, Father, calling to mind his death on
    the cross,
his perfect sacrifice made once for the sins
    of all men,
rejoicing at his mighty resurrection and
    glorious ascension,
and looking for his coming in glory,
we celebrate this memorial of our redemption;
We thank you for counting us worthy
to stand in your presence and serve you;
we bring before you this bread and this cup;

★ Alternative Acclamations

Dying you destroyed our death,
rising you restored our life.
Lord Jesus, come in glory.

When we eat this bread and drink this cup,
we proclaim your death, Lord Jesus,
until you come in glory.

Lord, by your cross and resurrection
you have set us free.
You are the Saviour of the world.

We pray you to accept this our duty and service,
a spiritual sacrifice of praise and thanksgiving;

Send the Holy Spirit on your people
and gather into one in your kingdom
all who share this one bread and one cup,
so that we, in the company of all the saints,
may praise and glorify you for ever,
through him from whom all good things come,
Jesus Christ our Lord;

By whom, and with whom, and in whom,
in the unity of the Holy Spirit,
all honour and glory be yours, almighty Father,
for ever and ever. **Amen.**

Silence may be kept.

FOURTH EUCHARISTIC PRAYER

| President | The Lord be with you or The Lord is here. |
| All | **and also with you.**   **His Spirit is with us.** |

President Lift up your hearts.
All **We lift them to the Lord.**

President Let us give thanks to the Lord our God.
All **It is right to give him thanks and praise.**

President It is indeed right,
it is our duty and our joy,
at all times and in all places
to give you thanks and praise,
holy Father, heavenly King,
almighty and eternal God,
creator of heaven and earth,
through Jesus Christ our Lord:

[PROPER PREFACE]

Therefore with angels and archangels,
and with all the company of heaven,

we proclaim your great and glorious name,
for ever praising you and saying:

All

Holy, holy, holy Lord,
God of power and might,
heaven and earth are full of your glory.
Hosanna in the highest.

THIS ANTHEM may also be used.

Blessed is he who comes in the name of
the Lord.
Hosanna in the highest.

President

All glory to you, our heavenly Father:
in your tender mercy
you gave your only Son Jesus Christ
to suffer death upon the cross for
    our redemption;
he made there
a full atonement for the sins of the whole world,
offering once for all his one sacrifice of himself;
he instituted,
and in his holy gospel commanded us
    to continue,
a perpetual memory of his precious death
until he comes again.

Hear us, merciful Father, we humbly pray,
and grant that by the power of your Holy Spirit
we who receive these gifts of your creation,
this bread and this wine,
according to your Son our Saviour Jesus Christ's
    holy institution,
in remembrance of the death that he suffered,
may be partakers of his most blessed body
    and blood;

Who in the same night that he was betrayed,
took bread and gave you thanks;

he broke it and gave it to his disciples, saying,
Take, eat; this is my body which is given for you;
do this in remembrance of me.
In the same way, after supper
he took the cup and gave you thanks;
he gave it to them, saying,

Drink this, all of you;
this is my blood of the new covenant,
which is shed for you and for many for the
    forgiveness of sins.
Do this, as often as you drink it,
in remembrance of me.

All ★ **Christ has died:**
Christ has risen:
Christ will come again.

President Therefore, Lord and heavenly Father,
in remembrance of the precious death
    and passion,
the mighty resurrection and glorious ascension
of your dear Son Jesus Christ,
we offer you through him this sacrifice of
    praise and thanksgiving.

★ Alternative Acclamations

Dying you destroyed our death,
rising you restored our life.
Lord Jesus, come in glory.

When we eat this bread and drink this cup,
we proclaim your death, Lord Jesus,
until you come in glory.

Lord, by your cross and resurrection
you have set us free.
You are the Saviour of the world.

Grant that by his merits and death,
and through faith in his blood,
we and all your Church may receive forgiveness
    of our sins
and all other benefits of his passion.
Although we are unworthy, through our
    many sins,
to offer you any sacrifice,
yet we pray that you will accept this,
the duty and service that we owe;
do not weigh our merits, but pardon
    our offences,
and fill us all who share in this
        holy communion
with your grace and heavenly blessing.

Through Jesus Christ our Lord,
by whom, and with whom, and in whom,
in the unity of the Holy Spirit,
all honour and glory be yours, almighty Father,
now and for ever.   **Amen.**

Silence may be kept.

THE PASSION NARRATIVES

THE PASSION NARRATIVES

THE PASSION NARRATIVES
IN CONTINUOUS FORM

The Passion Narratives are reproduced in full in the text of the Revised Standard Version.

References in the right-hand margin indicate the points at which readings begin and end on different days (see Lectionary, pp. 293–295).

▶ and ◀ indicate the beginning and end of the shortened Passion Reading appointed for Palm Sunday. If possible, however, the complete narrative should be used.

▷ and ◁ indicate the beginning and end of the Gospel of the Watch on Maundy Thursday.

Wherever the reading begins, it should be introduced by:
> The Passion of our Lord Jesus Christ according to *N*.

and where it ends, it should be followed by:
> This is the Passion of the Lord.

MATTHEW

Matthew 26 and 27

When Jesus had finished all these sayings, he said to his disciples, 'You know that after two days the Passover is coming, and the Son of man will be delivered up to be crucified.' 26.1

Then the chief priests and the elders of the people gathered in the palace of the high priest, who was called Caiaphas, and took counsel together in order to arrest Jesus by stealth and kill him. But they said, 'Not during the feast, lest there be a tumult among the people.'

Now when Jesus was at Bethany in the house of Simon the leper, a woman came up to him with an alabaster flask of very expensive ointment, and she poured it on his head, as he sat at table. But when the disciples saw it, they were indignant, saying, 'Why this waste? For this ointment might have been sold for a large sum, and given to the poor.' But Jesus, aware of this, said to them, 'Why do you trouble the woman? For she has done a beautiful thing to me. For you always have the poor with you, but you will not always have me. In pouring this ointment on my body she has done it to prepare me for burial. Truly, I say to you, wherever this gospel is preached in the whole world, what she has done will be told in memory of her.'

Then one of the twelve, who was called Judas Iscariot, went to the chief priests and said, 'What will you give me if I deliver him to you?' And they paid him thirty pieces of silver. And from that moment he sought an opportunity to betray him. Now on the first day of Unleavened Bread the disciples came to Jesus, saying, 'Where will you have us prepare for you to eat the passover?' He said, 'Go into the city to a certain one, and say to him, "The Teacher says, My time is at hand; I will keep the passover at your house with my disciples."' And the disciples did as Jesus had directed them, and they prepared the passover.

When it was evening, he sat at table with the twelve disciples; and as they were eating, he said, 'Truly, I say to you, one of you will betray me.' And they were very sorrowful, and began to say to him one after another, 'Is it I, Lord?' He answered, 'He who has dipped his hand in the dish with me, will betray me. The Son of man goes as it is written of him, but woe to that man by whom the Son of man is betrayed! It would have been better for that man if he had not been born.' Judas, who betrayed him, said, 'Is it I, Master?' He said to him, 'You have said so.'

Now as they were eating, Jesus took bread, and blessed, and broke it, and gave it to the disciples and said, 'Take, eat; this is my body.' And he took a cup, and when he had given thanks he gave it to them, saying, 'Drink of it, all of you; for this is my blood of the covenant, which is poured out for many for the forgiveness of sins. I tell you I shall not drink again of this fruit of the vine until that day when I drink it new with you in my Father's kingdom.'

▷ And when they had sung a hymn, they went out to the Mount →26.30→ of Olives. Then Jesus said to them, 'You will all fall away because 26.31→ of me this night; for it is written, "I will strike the shepherd, and the sheep of the flock will be scattered." But after I am raised up, I will go before you to Galilee.' Peter declared to him, 'Though they all fall away because of you, I will never fall away.' Jesus said to him, 'Truly, I say to you, this very night, before the cock crows, you will deny me three times.' Peter said to him, 'Even if I must die with you, I will not deny you.' And so said all the disciples.

► Then Jesus went with them to a place called Gethsemane, and 26.36→ he said to his disciples, 'Sit here, while I go yonder and pray.' And taking with him Peter and the two sons of Zebedee, he began to be sorrowful and troubled. Then he said to them, 'My soul is very sorrowful, even to death; remain here, and watch with me.' And going a little farther he fell on his face and prayed, 'My Father, if it be possible, let this cup pass from me; nevertheless, not as I will, but as you will.' And he came to the disciples and found them sleeping; and he said to Peter. 'So, could you not watch with me one hour? Watch and pray that you may not enter into temptation; the spirit indeed is willing, but the flesh is weak.' Again, for the second time, he went away and prayed, 'My Father, if this cannot pass unless I drink it, your will be done.' And again he came and found them sleeping, for their eyes were heavy. So, leaving them again, he went away and prayed for the third time, saying the same words. Then he came to the disciples and said to them, 'Are you still sleeping and taking your rest? Behold, the hour is at hand, and the Son of man is betrayed into the hands of sinners. Rise, let us be going; see, my betrayer is at hand.'

While he was still speaking, Judas came, one of the twelve, and with him a great crowd with swords and clubs, from the chief priests and the elders of the people. Now the betrayer had given them a sign, saying, 'The one I shall kiss is the man; seize him.' And he came up to Jesus at once and said, 'Hail, Master!' And he kissed him. Jesus said to him, 'Friend, why are you here?' Then they came up and laid hands on Jesus and seized him. And behold, one of those who were with Jesus stretched out his hand and drew his sword, and struck the slave of the high priest, and cut off his ear. Then Jesus said to him, 'Put your sword back into its place; for all who take the sword will perish by the sword. Do you think that I cannot appeal to my Father, and he will at once send me more than twelve legions of angels? But how then should the scriptures be fulfilled, that it must be so?' At that hour Jesus said to the crowds, 'Have you come out as against a robber, with swords and clubs to capture me? Day after day I sat in the temple teaching, and you did not seize me. But all this has taken place, that the scriptures of the prophets might be fulfilled.' Then all the disciples forsook him and fled.

Then those who had seized Jesus led him to Caiaphas the high priest, where the scribes and the elders had gathered. But Peter followed him at a distance, as far as the courtyard of the high priest, and going inside he sat with the guards to see the end. Now the chief priests and the whole council sought false testimony against Jesus that they might put him to death, but they found none, though many false witnesses came forward. At last two came forward and said, 'This fellow said, "I am able to destroy the temple of God, and to build it in three days."' And the high priest stood up and said, 'Have you no answer to make? What is it that these men testify against you?' But Jesus was silent. And the high priest said to him, 'I adjure you by the living God, tell us if you are the Christ, the Son of God.' Jesus said to him, 'You have said so. But I tell you, hereafter you will see the Son of man seated at the right hand of Power, and coming on the clouds of heaven.' Then the high priest tore his robes, and said, 'He has uttered blasphemy. Why do we still need witnesses? You have now heard his blasphemy. What is your judgment?' They answered, 'He deserves death.' Then they spat in his face, and struck him; and some slapped him, saying, 'Prophesy to us, you Christ! Who is it that struck you?'

Now Peter was sitting outside in the courtyard. And a maid came up to him, and said, 'You also were with Jesus the Galilean.' But he denied it before them all, saying, 'I do not know what you mean.' And when he went out to the porch, another maid saw him, and she said to the bystanders, 'This man was with Jesus of Nazareth.' And again he denied it with an oath, 'I do not know the man.' After a little while the bystanders came up and said to Peter, 'Certainly you are also one of them, for your accent betrays you.' Then he began to invoke a curse on himself and to swear, 'I do not know the man.' And immediately the cock crowed. And Peter remembered the saying of Jesus, 'Before the cock crows, you will deny me three times.' And he went out and wept bitterly. ◁ →26.75 (end)

27.1→

When morning came, all the chief priests and the elders of the people took counsel against Jesus to put him to death; and they bound him and led him away and delivered him to Pilate the governor.

When Judas, his betrayer, saw that he was condemned, he repented and brought back the thirty pieces of silver to the chief priests and the elders, saying, 'I have sinned in betraying innocent blood.' They said, 'What is that to us? See to it yourself.' And throwing down the pieces of silver in the temple, he departed; and he went and hanged himself. But the chief priests, taking the pieces of silver, said, 'It is not lawful to put them into the treasury, since they are blood money.' So they took counsel, and bought with them the potter's field, to bury strangers in. Therefore that field has been called the Field of Blood to this day. Then was fulfilled what had been spoken by the prophet Jeremiah, saying, 'And they took the thirty pieces of silver, the price of him on whom a price had been set by some of the sons of Israel, and they gave them for the potter's field, as the Lord directed me.'

Now Jesus stood before the governor; and the governor asked him, 'Are you the King of the Jews?' Jesus said, 'You have said so.' But when he was accused by the chief priests and elders, he made no answer. Then Pilate said to him, 'Do you not hear how many things they testify against you?' But he gave him no answer, not even to a single charge; so that the governor wondered greatly.

Now at the feast the governor was accustomed to release for the crowd any one prisoner whom they wanted. And they had then a notorious prisoner, called Barabbas. So when they had gathered, Pilate said to them, 'Whom do you want me to release for you, Barabbas or Jesus who is called Christ?' For he knew that it was out of envy that they had delivered him up. Besides, while he was sitting on the judgment seat, his wife sent word to him, 'Have nothing to do with that righteous man, for I have suffered much over him today in a dream.' Now the chief priests and the elders persuaded the people to ask for Barabbas and destroy Jesus. The governor again said to them, 'Which of the two do you want me to release for you?' And they said, 'Barabbas.' Pilate said to them, 'Then what shall I do with Jesus who is called Christ?' They all said, 'Let him be crucified.' And he said, 'Why, what evil has he done?' But they shouted all the more, 'Let him be crucified.'

So when Pilate saw that he was gaining nothing, but rather that a riot was beginning, he took water and washed his hands before the crowd, saying, 'I am innocent of this man's blood; see to it yourselves.' And all the people answered, 'His blood be on us and on our children!' Then he released for them Barabbas, and having scourged Jesus, delivered him to be crucified.

Then the soldiers of the governor took Jesus into the praetorium, and they gathered the whole battalion before him. And they stripped him and put a scarlet robe upon him, and plaiting a crown of thorns they put it on his head, and put a reed in his right hand. And kneeling before him they mocked him, saying, 'Hail, King of the Jews!' And they spat upon him, and took the reed and struck him on the head. And when they had mocked him, they stripped him of the robe, and put his own clothes on him, and led him away to crucify him.

As they went out, they came upon a man of Cyrene, Simon by name; this man they compelled to carry his cross. And when they came to a place called Golgotha (which means the place of a skull), they offered him wine to drink, mingled with gall; but when he tasted it, he would not drink it. And when they had crucified him, they divided his garments among them by casting lots; then they sat down and kept watch over him there. And over his head they put the charge against him, which read, 'This is Jesus the King of the Jews.' Then two robbers were crucified with him, one on the right and one on the left. And those who passed by derided him, wagging their heads and saying, 'You who would destroy the temple and build it in three days, save yourself! If you are the Son of God, come down from the cross.' So also the chief priests, with the scribes and elders, mocked him, saying, 'He saved others; he cannot save himself. He is the King of Israel; let him come down now from the cross, and we will believe in him. He trusts in God; let God deliver him now, if he desires him; for he said, "I am the Son of God."' And the robbers who were crucified with him also reviled him in the same way.

Now from the sixth hour there was darkness over all the land until the ninth hour. And about the ninth hour Jesus cried with a loud voice. 'Eli, Eli, lama sabachthani?' that is, 'My God, my God, why have you forsaken me?' And some of the bystanders hearing it said, 'This man is calling Elijah.' And one of them at once ran and took a sponge, filled it with vinegar, and put it on a reed, and gave it to him to drink. But the others said, 'Wait, let us see whether Elijah will come to save him.' And Jesus cried again with a loud voice and yielded up his spirit.

And behold, the curtain of the temple was torn in two, from top to bottom; and the earth shook, and the rocks were split; the tombs also were opened, and many bodies of the saints who had fallen asleep were raised, and coming out of the tombs after his resurrection they went into the holy city and appeared to many. When the centurion and those who were with him, keeping watch over Jesus, saw the earthquake and what took place, they were filled with awe, and said, 'Truly this was the Son of God!' ◀ →27

There were also many women there, looking on from afar, who had followed Jesus from Galilee, ministering to him; among whom were Mary Magdalene, and Mary the mother of James and Joseph, and the mother of the sons of Zebedee.

When it was evening, there came a rich man from Arimathea, named Joseph, who also was a disciple of Jesus. He went to Pilate and asked for the body of Jesus. Then Pilate ordered it to be given to him. And Joseph took the body, and wrapped it in a clean linen shroud, and laid it in his own new tomb, which he had hewn in the rock; and he rolled a great stone to the door of the tomb, and departed. Mary Magdalene and the other Mary were there, sitting opposite the sepulchre.

Next day, that is, after the day of Preparation, the chief priests and the Pharisees gathered before Pilate and said, 'Sir, we remember how that impostor said, while he was still alive, "After three days I will rise again." Therefore order the sepulchre to be made secure until the third day, lest his disciples go and steal him away, and tell the people, "He has risen from the dead," and the last fraud will be worse than the first.' Pilate said to them, 'You have a guard of soldiers; go, make it as secure as you can.' So they went and made the sepulchre secure by sealing the stone and setting a guard.

MARK

Mark 14 and 15

It was now two days before the Passover and the feast of 14.1→ Unleavened Bread. And the chief priests and the scribes were seeking how to arrest Jesus by stealth, and kill him; for they said, 'Not during the feast, lest there be a tumult of the people.'

And while he was at Bethany in the house of Simon the leper, as he sat at table, a woman came with an alabaster flask of ointment of pure nard, very costly, and she broke the flask and poured it over his head. But there were some who said to themselves indignantly, 'Why was the ointment thus wasted? For this ointment might have been sold for more than three hundred denarii, and given to the poor.' And they reproached her. But Jesus said, 'Let her alone; why do you trouble her? She has done a beautiful thing to me. For you always have the poor with you, and whenever you will, you can do good to them; but you will not always have me. She has done what she could; she has anointed my body beforehand for burying. And truly, I say to you, wherever the gospel is preached in the whole world, what she has done will be told in memory of her.'

Then Judas Iscariot, who was one of the twelve, went to the chief priests in order to betray him to them. And when they heard it they were glad, and promised to give him money. And he sought an opportunity to betray him.

And on the first day of Unleavened Bread, when they sacrificed the passover lamb, his disciples said to him, 'Where you will have us go and prepare for you to eat the passover?' And he sent two of his disciples, and said to them, 'Go into the city, and a man carrying a jar of water will meet you; follow him, and wherever he enters, say to the householder, "The Teacher says, Where is my guest room, where I am to eat the passover with my disciples?" And he will show you a large upper room furnished and ready; there prepare for us.' And the disciples set out and went to the city, and found it as he had told them; and they prepared the passover.

And when it was evening he came with the twelve. And as they were at table eating, Jesus said, 'Truly, I say to you, one of you will betray me, one who is eating with me.' They began to be sorrowful, and to say to him one after another, 'Is it I?' He said to them, 'It is one of the twelve, one who is dipping bread into the dish with me. For the Son of man goes as it is written of him, but woe to that man by whom the Son of man is betrayed! It would have been better for that man if he had not been born.'

And as they were eating, he took bread, and blessed, and broke it, and gave it to them, and said, 'Take; this is my body.' And he took a cup, and when he had given thanks he gave it to them, and they all drank of it. And he said to them, 'This is my blood of the covenant, which is poured out for many. Truly, I say to you, I shall not drink again of the fruit of the vine until that day when I drink it new in the kingdom of God.'

▷ And when they had sung a hymn, they went out to the Mount of Olives. And Jesus said to them, 'You will all fall away; for it is written, "I will strike the shepherd, and the sheep will be scattered." But after I am raised up, I will go before you to Galilee.' Peter said to him. 'Even though they all fall away, I will not.' And Jesus said to him, 'Truly, I say to you, this very night, before the cock crows twice, you will deny me three times.' But he said vehemently, 'If I must die with you, I will not deny you.' And they all said the same. →14.

▶ And they went to a place which was called Gethsemane; and he said to his disciples, 'Sit here, while I pray.' And he took with him Peter and James and John, and began to be greatly distressed and troubled. And he said to them, 'My soul is very sorrowful, even to death; remain here, and watch.' And going a little farther, he fell on the ground and prayed that, if it were possible, the hour might pass from him. And he said, 'Abba, Father, all things are possible to you; remove this cup from me; yet not what I will, but what you will.' And he came and found them sleeping, and he

14.26
14.32

said to Peter, 'Simon, are you asleep? Could you not watch one hour? Watch and pray that you may not enter into temptation; the spirit indeed is willing, but the flesh is weak.' And again he went away and prayed, saying the same words. And again he came and found them sleeping, for their eyes were very heavy; and they did not know what to answer him. And he came the third time, and said to them, 'Are you still sleeping and taking your rest? It is enough; the hour has come; the Son of man is betrayed into the hands of sinners. Rise, let us be going; see, my betrayer is at hand.'

And immediately, while he was still speaking, Judas came, one of the twelve, and with him a crowd with swords and clubs, from the chief priests and the scribes and the elders. Now the betrayer had given them a sign, saying, 'The one I shall kiss is the man; seize him and lead him away under guard.' And when he came, he went up to him at once, and said, 'Master!' And he kissed him. And they laid hands on him and seized him. But one of those who stood by drew his sword, and struck the slave of the high priest and cut off his ear. And Jesus said to them, 'Have you come out as against a robber, with swords and clubs to capture me? Day after day I was with you in the temple teaching, and you did not seize me. But let the scriptures be fulfilled.' And they all forsook him, and fled.

And a young man followed him, with nothing but a linen cloth about his body; and they seized him, but he left the linen cloth and ran away naked.

And they led Jesus to the high priest; and all the chief priests and the elders and the scribes were assembled. And Peter had followed him at a distance, right into the courtyard of the high priest; and he was sitting with the guards, and warming himself at the fire. Now the chief priests and the whole council sought testimony against Jesus to put him to death; but they found none. For many bore false witness against him, and their witness did not agree. And some stood up and bore false witness against him, saying, 'We heard him say, "I will destroy this temple that is made with hands, and in three days I will build another, not made with hands."' Yet not even so did their testimony agree. And the high priest stood up in the midst, and asked Jesus, 'Have you no answer to make? What is it that these men testify against you?' But he was silent and made no answer. Again the high priest asked him, 'Are you the Christ, the Son of the Blessed?' And Jesus said, 'I am; and you will see the Son of man seated at the right hand of Power, and coming with the clouds of heaven.' And the high priest tore his garments, and said, 'Why do we still need witnesses? You have heard his blasphemy. What is your decision?' And they all condemned him as deserving death. And some began to spit on him, and to cover his face, and to strike him, saying to him, 'Prophesy!' And the guards received him with blows.

And as Peter was below in the courtyard, one of the maids of the high priest came; and seeing Peter warming himself, she looked at him, and said, 'You also were with the Nazarene, Jesus.' But he denied it, saying, 'I neither know nor understand what you mean.' And he went out into the gateway. And the maid saw him, and began again to say to the bystanders, 'This man is one of them.' But again he denied it. And after a little while again the bystanders said to Peter, 'Certainly you are one of them, for you are a Galilean.' But he began to invoke a curse on himself and to swear, 'I do not know this man of whom you speak.' And immediately the cock crowed a second time. And Peter remembered how Jesus had said to him, 'Before the cock crows twice, you will deny me three times.' And he broke down and wept. ◁

→14.72 (en

15.1
As soon as it was morning the chief priests, with the elders and scribes, and the whole council held a consultation; and they bound Jesus and led him away and delivered him to Pilate. And Pilate asked him, 'Are you the King of the Jews?' And he answered him, 'You have said so.' And the chief priests accused him of many things. And Pilate again asked him, 'Have you no answer to make? See how many charges they bring against you.' But Jesus made no further answer, so that Pilate wondered.

Now at the feast he used to release for them one prisoner for whom they asked. And among the rebels in prison, who had committed murder in the insurrection, there was a man called Barabbas. And the crowd came up and began to ask Pilate to do as he was wont to do for them. And he answered them, 'Do you want me to release for you the King of the Jews?' For he perceived that it was out of envy that the chief priests had delivered him up. But the chief priests stirred up the crowd to have him release for them Barabbas instead. And Pilate again said to them, 'Then what shall I do with the man whom you call the King of the Jews?' And they cried out again, 'Crucify him.' And Pilate said to them, 'Why, what evil has he done?' But they shouted all the more, 'Crucify him.' So Pilate, wishing to satisfy the crowd, released for them Barabbas; and having scourged Jesus, he delivered him to be crucified.

And the soldiers led him away inside the palace (that is, the praetorium); and they called together the whole battalion. And they clothed him in a purple cloak, and plaiting a crown of thorns they put it on him. And they began to salute him, 'Hail, King of the Jews!' And they struck his head with a reed, and spat upon him, and they knelt down in homage to him. And when they had mocked him, they stripped him of the purple cloak, and put his own clothes on him. And they led him out to crucify him.

And they compelled a passer-by, Simon of Cyrene, who was coming in from the country, the father of Alexander and Rufus, to carry his cross. And they brought him to the place called Golgotha (which means the place of a skull). And they offered him wine mingled with myrrh; but he did not take it. And they crucified him, and divided his garments among them, casting lots for them, to decide what each should take. And it was the third hour, when they crucified him. And the inscription of the charge against him read, 'The King of the Jews.' And with him they crucified two robbers, one on his right and one on his left. And those who passed by derided him, wagging their heads, and saying, 'Aha! You who would destroy the temple and build it in three days, save yourself, and come down from the cross!' So also the chief priests mocked him to one another with the scribes, saying, 'He saved others; he cannot save himself. Let the Christ, the King of Israel, come down now from the cross, that we may see and believe.' Those who were crucified with him also reviled him.

And when the sixth hour had come, there was darkness over the whole land until the ninth hour. And at the ninth hour Jesus cried with a loud voice, 'Eloi, Eloi, lama sabachthani?' which means, 'My God, my God, why have you forsaken me?' And some of the bystanders hearing it said, 'Behold, he is calling Elijah.' And one ran and, filling a sponge full of vinegar, put it on a reed and gave it to him to drink, saying, 'Wait, let us see whether Elijah will come to take him down.' And Jesus uttered a loud cry, and breathed his last. And the curtain of the temple was torn in two, from top to bottom. And when the centurion, who stood facing him, saw that he thus breathed his last, he said, 'Truly this man was the Son of God!' ◀︎

→15

There were also women looking on from afar, among whom were Mary Magdalene, and Mary the mother of James the younger and of Joses, and Salome, who, when he was in Galilee, followed him, and ministered to him; and also many other women who came up with him to Jerusalem.

And when evening had come, since it was the day of Preparation, that is, the day before the sabbath, Joseph of Arimathea, a respected member of the council, who was also himself looking for the kingdom of God, took courage and went to Pilate, and asked for the body of Jesus. And Pilate wondered if he were already dead; and summoning the centurion, he asked him whether he was already dead. And when he learned from the centurion that he was dead, he granted the body to Joseph. And he bought a linen shroud, and taking him down, wrapped him in the linen shroud, and laid him in a tomb which had been hewn out of the rock; and he rolled a stone against the door of the tomb. Mary Magdalene and Mary the mother of Joses saw where he was laid.

LUKE

Luke 22 and 23

Now the feast of Unleavened Bread drew near, which is called the Passover. And the chief priests and the scribes were seeking how to put him to death; for they feared the people.

22.1→

Then Satan entered into Judas called Iscariot, who was of the number of the twelve; he went away and conferred with the chief priests and officers how he might betray him to them. And they were glad, and engaged to give him money. So he agreed, and sought an opportunity to betray him to them in the absence of the multitude.

Then came the day of Unleavened Bread, on which the passover lamb had to be sacrificed. So Jesus sent Peter and John, saying, 'Go and prepare the passover for us, that we may eat it.' They said to him, 'Where will you have us prepare it?' He said to them, 'Behold, when you have entered the city, a man carrying a jar of water will meet you; follow him into the house which he enters, and tell the householder, "The Teacher says to you, Where is the guest room, where I am to eat the passover with my disciples?" And he will show you a large upper room furnished; there make ready.' And they went, and found it as he had told them; and they prepared the passover.

And when the hour came, he sat at table, and the apostles with him. And he said to them, 'I have earnestly desired to eat this passover with you before I suffer; for I tell you I shall not eat it until it is fulfilled in the kingdom of God.' And he took a cup, and when he had given thanks he said, 'Take this, and divide it among yourselves; for I tell you that from now on I shall not drink of the fruit of the vine until the kingdom of God comes.' And he took bread, and when he had given thanks he broke it and gave it to them, saying, 'This is my body which is given for you. Do this in remembrance of me.' And likewise the cup after supper, saying, 'This cup which is poured out for you is the new covenant in my blood. But behold the hand of him who betrays me is with me on the table. For the Son of man goes as it has been determined; but woe to that man by whom he is betrayed!' And they began to question one another, which of them it was that would do this.

A dispute also arose among them, which of them was to be regarded as the greatest. And he said to them, 'The kings of the Gentiles exercise lordship over them; and those in authority over them are called benefactors. But not so with you; rather let the greatest among you become as the youngest, and the leader as one who serves. For which is the greater, one who sits at table, or one who serves? Is it not the one who sits at table? But I am among you as one who serves.

'You are those who have continued with me in my trials; and I assign to you, as my Father assigned to me, a kingdom, that you may eat and drink at my table in my kingdom, and sit on thrones judging the twelve tribes of Israel.

▷ 'Simon, Simon, behold, Satan demanded to have you, that he might sift you like wheat, but I have prayed for you that your faith may not fail; and when you have turned again, strengthen your brethren.' 22.3

And he said to him, 'Lord, I am ready to go with you to prison and to death.' He said, 'I tell you, Peter, the cock will not crow this day, until you three times deny that you know me.'

And he said to them, 'When I sent you out with no purse or bag or sandals, did you lack anything?' They said, 'Nothing.' He said to them, 'But now, let him who has a purse take it, and likewise a bag. And let him who has no sword sell his mantle and buy one. For I tell you that this scripture must be fulfilled in me, "And he was reckoned with transgressors"; for what is written about me has its fulfilment.' And they said, 'Look, Lord, here are two swords.' And he said to them, 'It is enough.' →22

▶ And he came out, and went, as was his custom, to the Mount of Olives; and the disciples followed him. And when he came to the place he said to them, 'Pray that you may not enter into temptation.' And he withdrew from them about a stone's throw, 22.3

and knelt down and prayed, 'Father, if you are willing, remove this cup from me; nevertheless not my will, but yours, be done.' And when he rose from prayer, he came to the disciples and found them sleeping for sorrow, and he said to them, 'Why do you sleep? Rise and pray that you may not enter into temptation.'

While he was still speaking, there came a crowd, and the man called Judas, one of the twelve, was leading them. He drew near to Jesus to kiss him; but Jesus said to him, 'Judas, would you betray the Son of man with a kiss?' And when those who were about him saw what would follow, they said, 'Lord, shall we strike with the sword?' And one of them struck the slave of the high priest and cut off his right ear. But Jesus said, 'No more of this!' And he touched his ear and healed him. Then Jesus said to the chief priests and officers of the temple and elders, who had come out against him, 'Have you come out as against a robber, with swords and clubs? When I was with you day after day in the temple, you did not lay hands on me. But this is your hour, and the power of darkness.'

Then they seized him and led him away, bringing him into the high priest's house. Peter followed at a distance; and when they had kindled a fire in the middle of the courtyard and sat down together, Peter sat among them. Then a maid, seeing him as he sat in the light and gazing at him, said, 'This man also was with him.' But he denied it, saying, 'Woman, I do not know him.' And a little later some one else saw him and said, 'You also are one of them.' But Peter said, 'Man, I am not.' And after an interval of about an hour still another insisted, saying, 'Certainly this man also was with him; for he is a Galilean.' But Peter said, 'Man, I do not know what you are saying.' And immediately, while he was still speaking, the cock crowed. And the Lord turned and looked at Peter. And Peter remembered the word of the Lord, how he had said to him, 'Before the cock crows today, you will deny me three times.' And he went out and wept bitterly. ◁

→22.62

Now the men who were holding Jesus mocked him and beat him; they also blindfolded him and asked him, 'Prophesy! Who is it that struck you?' And they spoke many other words against him, reviling him.

→22.

When day came, the assembly of the elders of the people gathered together, both chief priests and scribes; and they led him away to their council, and they said, 'If you are the Christ, tell us.' But he said to them, 'If I tell you, you will not believe; and if I ask you, you will not answer. But from now on the Son of man shall be seated at the right hand of the power of God.' And they all said, 'Are you the Son of God, then?' And he said to them, 'You say that I am.' And they said, 'What further testimony do we need? We have heard it ourselves from his own lips.' Then the whole company of them arose, and brought him before Pilate. And they began to accuse him, saying, 'We found this man perverting our nation, and forbidding us to give tribute to Caesar, and saying that he himself is Christ a king.' And Pilate asked him, 'Are you the King of the Jews?' And he answered him, 'You have said so.' And Pilate said to the chief priests and the multitudes, 'I find no crime in this man.' But they were urgent, saying, 'He stirs up the people, teaching throughout all Judea, from Galilee even to this place.'

When Pilate heard this, he asked whether the man was a Galilean. And when he learned that he belonged to Herod's jurisdiction, he sent him over to Herod, who was himself in Jerusalem at the time. When Herod saw Jesus, he was very glad, for he had long desired to see him, because he had heard about him, and he was hoping to see some sign done by him. So he questioned him at some length; but he made no answer. The chief priests and the scribes stood by, vehemently accusing him. And Herod with his soldiers treated him with contempt and mocked him; then, arraying him in gorgeous apparel, he sent him back to Pilate. And Herod and Pilate became friends with each other that very day, for before this they had been at enmity with each other.

Pilate then called together the chief priests and the rulers and the people, and said to them, 'You brought me this man as one who was perverting the people; and after examining him before you, behold, I did not find this man guilty of any of your charges against him; neither did Herod, for he sent him back to us. Behold, nothing deserving death has been done by him; I will therefore chastise him and release him.'

But they all cried out together, 'Away with this man, and release to us Barabbas' – a man who had been thrown into prison for an insurrection started in the city, and for murder. Pilate addressed them once more, desiring to release Jesus; but they shouted out, 'Crucify, crucify him!' A third time he said to them, 'Why, what evil has he done? I have found in him no crime deserving death; I will therefore chastise him and release him.' But they were urgent, demanding with loud cries that he should be crucified. And their voices prevailed. So Pilate gave sentence that their demand should be granted. He released the man who had been thrown into prison for insurrection and murder, whom they asked for; but Jesus he delivered up to their will.

And as they led him away, they seized one Simon of Cyrene, who was coming in from the country, and laid on him the cross, to carry it behind Jesus. And there followed him a great multitude of the people, and of women who bewailed and lamented him. But Jesus turning to them said, 'Daughters of Jerusalem, do not weep for me, but weep for yourselves and for your children. For behold, the days are coming when they will say, "Blessed are the barren, and the wombs that never bore, and the breasts that never gave suck!" Then they will begin to say to the mountains, "Fall on us"; and to the hills, "Cover us." For if they do this when the wood is green, what will happen when it is dry?'

Two others also, who were criminals, were led away to be put to death with him. And when they came to the place which is called The Skull, there they crucified him, and the criminals, one on the right and one on the left. And Jesus said, 'Father, forgive them; for they know not what they do.' And they cast lots to divide his garments. And the people stood by, watching; but the rulers scoffed at him, saying, 'He saved others; let him save himself, if he is the Christ of God, his Chosen One!' The soldiers also mocked him, coming up and offering him vinegar, and saying, 'If you are the King of the Jews, save yourself!' There was also an inscription over him, 'This is the King of the Jews.'

One of the criminals who were hanged railed at him, saying, 'Are you not the Christ? Save yourself and us!' But the other rebuked him, saying, 'Do you not fear God, since you are under the same sentence of condemnation? And we indeed justly; for we are receiving the due reward of our deeds; but this man has done nothing wrong.' And he said, 'Jesus, remember me when you come into your kingdom.' And he said to him, 'Truly, I say to you, today you will be with me in Paradise.'

It was now about the sixth hour, and there was darkness over the whole land until the ninth hour, while the sun's light failed; and the curtain of the temple was torn in two. Then Jesus, crying with a loud voice, said, 'Father, into your hands I commit my spirit!' And having said this he breathed his last. Now when the centurion saw what had taken place, he praised God, and said, 'Certainly this man was innocent!' And all the multitudes who assembled to see the sight, when they saw what had taken place, returned home beating their breasts. ◄

→23.◄

And all his acquaintances and the women who had followed him from Galilee stood at a distance and saw these things.

Now there was a man named Joseph from the Jewish town of Arimathea. He was a member of the council, a good and righteous man, who had not consented to their purpose and deed, and he was looking for the kingdom of God. This man went to Pilate and asked for the body of Jesus. Then he took it down and wrapped it in a linen shroud, and laid him in a rock-hewn tomb, where no one had ever yet been laid. It was the day of Preparation, and the sabbath was beginning. The women who had come with him from Galilee followed, and saw the tomb, and how his body was laid; then they returned, and prepared spices and ointments.

On the sabbath they rested according to the commandment.

JOHN

John 18 and 19

Jesus went forth with his disciples across the Kidron valley, where 18.1→ there was a garden, which he and his disciples entered. Now Judas, who betrayed him, also knew the place; for Jesus often met there with his disciples. So Judas, procuring a band of soldiers and some officers from the chief priests and the Pharisees, went there with lanterns and torches and weapons. Then Jesus, knowing all that was to befall him, came forward and said to them, 'Whom do you seek?' They answered him, 'Jesus of Nazareth.' Jesus said to them, 'I am he.' Judas, who betrayed him, was standing with them. When he said to them, 'I am he,' they drew back and fell to the ground. Again he asked them, 'Whom do you seek?' And they said, 'Jesus of Nazareth.' Jesus answered, 'I told you that I am he; so if you seek me, let these men go.' This was to fulfil the word which he had spoken, 'Of those whom you gave me I lost not one.' Then Simon Peter, having a sword, drew it and struck the high priest's slave and cut off his right ear. The slave's name was Malchus. Jesus said to Peter, 'Put your sword into its sheath; shall I not drink the cup which the Father has given me?'

So the band of soldiers and their captain and the officers of the Jews seized Jesus and bound him. First they led him to Annas; for he was the father-in-law of Caiaphas, who was high priest that year. It was Caiaphas who had given counsel to the Jews that it was expedient that one man should die for the people.

Simon Peter followed Jesus, and so did another disciple. As this disciple was known to the high priest, he entered the court of the high priest along with Jesus, while Peter stood outside at the door. So the other disciple, who was known to the high priest, went out and spoke to the maid who kept the door, and brought Peter in. The maid who kept the door said to Peter, 'Are not you also one of this man's disciples?' He said, 'I am not.' Now the servants and officers had made a charcoal fire, because it was cold, and they were standing and warming themselves; Peter also was with them, standing and warming himself.

The high priest then questioned Jesus about his disciples and his teaching. Jesus answered him, 'I have spoken openly to the world; I have always taught in synagogues and in the temple, where all Jews come together; I have said nothing secretly. Why do you ask me? Ask those who have heard me, what I said to them; they know what I said.' When he had said this, one of the officers standing by struck Jesus with his hand, saying, 'Is that how you answer the high priest?' Jesus answered him, 'If I have spoken wrongly, bear witness to the wrong; but if I have spoken rightly, why do you strike me?' Annas then sent him bound to Caiaphas the high priest.

Now Simon Peter was standing and warming himself. They said to him, 'Are not you also one of his disciples?' He denied it and said, 'I am not.' One of the servants of the high priest, a kinsman of the man whose ear Peter had cut off, asked, 'Did I not see you in the garden with him?' Peter again denied it; and at once the cock crowed.

Then they led Jesus from the house of Caiaphas to the praetorium. It was early. They themselves did not enter the praetorium, so that they might not be defiled, but might eat the passover. So Pilate went out to them and said, 'What accusation do you bring against this man?' They answered him, 'If this man were not an evildoer, we would not have handed him over.' Pilate said to them, 'Take him yourselves and judge him by your own law.' The Jews said to him, 'It is not lawful for us to put any man to death.' This was to fulfil the word which Jesus had spoken to show by what death he was to die.

Pilate entered the praetorium again and called Jesus, and said to him, 'Are you the King of the Jews?' Jesus answered, 'Do you say this of your own accord, or did others say it to you about me?' Pilate answered, 'Am I a Jew? Your own nation and the chief priests have handed you over to me; what have you done?' Jesus answered, 'My kingship is not of this world; if my kingship were of this world, my servants would fight, that I might not be handed over to the Jews; but my kingship is not from the world.' Pilate said to him, 'So you are a king?' Jesus answered, 'You say that I am a king. For this I was born, and for this I have come into the world, to bear witness to the truth. Every one who is of the truth hears my voice.' Pilate said to him, 'What is truth?'

After he had said this, he went out to the Jews again, and told them, 'I find no crime in him. But you have a custom that I should release one man for you at the Passover; will you have me release for you the King of the Jews?' They cried out again, 'Not this man, but Barabbas!' Now Barabbas was a robber.

Then Pilate took Jesus and scourged him. And the soldiers plaited a crown of thorns, and put it on his head, and arrayed him in a purple robe; they came up to him, saying, 'Hail, King of the Jews!' and struck him with their hands. Pilate went out again, and said to them, 'See, I am bringing him out to you, that you may know that I find no crime in him.' So Jesus came out, wearing the crown of thorns and the purple robe. Pilate said to them, 'Behold the man!' When the chief priests and the officers saw him, they cried out, 'Crucify him, crucify him!' Pilate said to them, 'Take him yourselves and crucify him, for I find no crime in him.' The Jews answered him, 'We have a law, and by that law he ought to die, because he has made himself the Son of God.' When Pilate heard these words, he was the more afraid; he entered the praetorium again and said to Jesus, 'Where are you from?' But Jesus gave no answer. Pilate therefore said to him, 'You will not speak to me? Do you not know that I have power to release you, and power to crucify you?' Jesus answered him, 'You would have no power over me unless it had been given you from above; therefore he who delivered me to you has the greater sin.'

Upon this Pilate sought to release him, but the Jews cried out, 'If you release this man, you are not Caesar's friend; every one who makes himself a king sets himself against Caesar.' When Pilate heard these words, he brought Jesus out and sat down on the judgement seat at a place called The Pavement, and in Hebrew,

Gabbatha. Now it was the day of Preparation of the Passover; it was about the sixth hour. He said to the Jews, 'Behold your King!' They cried out, 'Away with him, away with him, crucify him!' Pilate said to them, 'Shall I crucify your King?' The chief priests answered, 'We have no king but Caesar.' Then he handed him over to them to be crucified.

So they took Jesus, and he went out, bearing his own cross, to the place called the place of a skull, which is called in Hebrew Golgotha. There they crucified him, and with him two others, one on either side, and Jesus between them. Pilate also wrote a title and put it on the cross; it read, 'Jesus of Nazareth, the King of the Jews.' Many of the Jews read this title, for the place where Jesus was crucified was near the city; and it was written in Hebrew, in Latin, and in Greek. The chief priests of the Jews then said to Pilate, Do not write, 'The King of the Jews', but, 'This man said, "I am King of the Jews."' Pilate answered, 'What I have written I have written.'

When the soldiers had crucified Jesus they took his garments and made four parts, one for each soldier; also his tunic. But the tunic was without seam, woven from top to bottom; so they said to one another, 'Let us not tear it, but cast lots for it to see whose it shall be.' This was to fulfil the scripture,

'They parted my garments among them,
and for my clothing they cast lots.'
So the soldiers did this. But standing by the cross of Jesus were his mother, and his mother's sister, Mary the wife of Clopas, and Mary Magdalene. When Jesus saw his mother, and the disciple whom he loved standing near, he said to his mother, 'Woman, behold, your son!' Then he said to the disciple, 'Behold, your mother!' And from that hour the disciple took her to his own home.

After this Jesus, knowing that all was now finished, said (to fulfil the scripture), 'I thirst.' A bowl full of vinegar stood there; so they put a sponge full of the vinegar on hyssop and held it to his mouth. When Jesus had received the vinegar, he said, 'It is finished'; and he bowed his head and gave up his spirit.

Since it was the day of Preparation, in order to prevent the bodies from remaining on the cross on the sabbath (for that sabbath was a high day), the Jews asked Pilate that their legs might be broken, and that they might be taken away. So the soldiers came and broke the legs of the first, and of the other who had been crucified with him; but when they came to Jesus and saw that he was already dead, they did not break his legs. But one of the soldiers pierced his side with a spear, and at once there came out blood and water. He who saw it has borne witness – his testimony is true, and he knows that he tells the truth – that you also may believe. For these things took place that the scripture might be fulfilled, 'Not a bone of him shall be broken.' And again another scripture says, 'They shall look on him whom they have pierced.' →19.37

After this Joseph of Arimathea, who was a disciple of Jesus, but secretly, for fear of the Jews, asked Pilate that he might take away the body of Jesus, and Pilate gave him leave. So he came and took away his body. Nicodemus also, who had at first come to him by night, came bringing a mixture of myrrh and aloes, about a hundred pounds' weight. They took the body of Jesus, and bound it in linen cloths with the spices, as is the burial custom of the Jews. Now in the place where he was crucified there was a garden, and in the garden a new tomb where no one had ever been laid. So because of the Jewish day of Preparation, as the tomb was close at hand, they laid Jesus there.

THE PASSION NARRATIVES
IN DRAMATIC FORM

The narratives of the Passion according to the four evangelists are here set out for reading by several voices. The text used is that of the Revised Standard Version.

References in the right-hand margin indicate the points at which readings begin and end on different days (see Lectionary, pp. 293–295).

▶ and ◀ indicate the beginning and end of the shortened Passion Reading appointed for Palm Sunday. If possible, however, the complete narrative should be used.

▷ and ◁ indicate the beginning and end of the Gospel of the Watch on Maundy Thursday.

Wherever the reading begins, it should be introduced by:
> The Passion of our Lord Jesus Christ according to *N*.

and where it ends, it should be followed by:
> This is the Passion of the Lord.

MATTHEW

Matthew 26 and 27

Evangelist	When Jesus had finished all these sayings, he said to his disciples:
Jesus	You know that after two days the Passover is coming, and the Son of man will be delivered up to be crucified.
Evangelist	Then the chief priests and the elders of the people gathered in the palace of the high priest, who was called Caiaphas, and took counsel together in order to arrest Jesus by stealth and kill him. But they said:
Priests	Not during the feast, lest there be a tumult among the people.
Evangelist	Now when Jesus was at Bethany in the house of Simon the leper, a woman came up to him with an alabaster jar of very expensive ointment, and she poured it on his head, as he sat at table. But when the disciples saw it, they were indignant:
Disciples	Why this waste? For this ointment might have been sold for a large sum, and given to the poor.
Evangelist	But Jesus, aware of this, said to them:
Jesus	Why do you trouble this woman? She has done a beautiful thing for me. For you always have the poor with you, but you will not always have me. In pouring this ointment on my body she has done it to prepare me for burial. Truly, I say to you, wherever this gospel is preached in the whole world, what she has done will be told in memory of her.
Evangelist	Then one of the twelve, who was called Judas Iscariot, went to the chief priests and said:
Judas	What will you give me if I deliver Jesus to you?
Evangelist	And they paid him thirty pieces of silver. And from that moment he sought an opportunity to betray him.

26.1→

Now on the first day of Unleavened Bread the disciples came to Jesus:

Disciples   Where will you have us prepare for you to eat the passover?

Jesus   Go into the city to a certain one, and say to him, 'The Teacher says, "My time is at hand; I will keep the passover at your house with my disciples." '

Evangelist   And the disciples did as Jesus had directed them, and they prepared the Passover.

When it was evening, he sat at table with the twelve disciples; and as they were eating, he said:

Jesus   Truly I say to you, one of you will betray me.

Evangelist   And they were very sorrowful, and began to say to him one after another:

Disciples   Is it I, Lord?

Jesus   He who has dipped his hand in the dish with me, will betray me. The Son of man goes as it is written of him, but woe to that man by whom the Son of man is betrayed! It would have been better for that man if he had not been born.

Evangelist   Judas, who betrayed him, said:

Judas   Is it I, Master?

Jesus   You have said so.

Evangelist   Now as they were eating, Jesus took bread, and blessed, and broke it, and gave it to the disciples and said:

Jesus   Take, eat; this is my body.

Evangelist   And he took a cup, and when he had given thanks he gave it to them, saying:

Jesus   Drink of it, all of you; for this is my blood of the covenant, which is poured out for many for the forgiveness of sins. I tell you I shall not drink again of this fruit of the vine until that day when I drink it new with you in my Father's kingdom.

Evangelist   ▷ When they had sung a hymn, Jesus and the disciples went out to the Mount of Olives. →26.30
Then Jesus said to them: 26.31→

Jesus	You will all fall away because of me this night; for it is written, 'I will strike the shepherd, and the sheep of the flock will be scattered'. But after I am raised up, I will go before you to Galilee.
Evangelist	Peter declared to him:
Peter	Though they all fall away because of you, I will never fall away.
Jesus	Truly, I say to you, this very night, before the cock crows, you will deny me three times.
Peter	Even if I must die with you, I will not deny you.
Evangelist	And so said all the disciples.
	▶ Then Jesus went with them to a place called Gethsemane, and he said to his disciples:
Jesus	Sit here, while I go yonder and pray.
Evangelist	And taking with him Peter and the two sons of Zebedee, he began to be sorrowful and troubled. Then he said to them:
Jesus	My soul is very sorrowful, even to death; remain here and watch with me.
Evangelist	And going a little farther he fell on his face and prayed:
Jesus	My Father, if it be possible, let this cup pass from me; nevertheless, not as I will, but as you will.
Evangelist	And he came to the disciples and found them sleeping; and he said to Peter:
Jesus	So, could you not watch with me one hour? Watch and pray that you may not enter into temptation; the spirit indeed is willing, but the flesh is weak.
Evangelist	Again, for the second time, he went away and prayed:
Jesus	My Father, if this cannot pass unless I drink it, your will be done.
Evangelist	And again he came and found them sleeping, for their eyes were heavy. So, leaving them again, he went away and prayed for the third time, saying the same words. Then he came to the disciples and said to them:

26.36→

Jesus	Are you still sleeping and taking your rest? Behold, the hour is at hand, and the Son of man is betrayed into the hands of sinners. Rise, let us be going; see, my betrayer is at hand.
Evangelist	While he was still speaking, Judas came, one of the twelve, and with him a great crowd with swords and clubs, from the chief priests and the elders of the people. Now the betrayer had given them a sign:
Judas	The one I shall kiss is the man; seize him.
Evangelist	And he came up to Jesus at once.
Judas	Hail, Master!
Evangelist	And he kissed him.
Jesus	Friend, why are you here?
Evangelist	Then they came up and laid hands on Jesus and seized him. And behold, one of those who were with Jesus stretched out his hand and drew his sword, and struck the slave of the high priest, and cut off his ear.
Jesus	Put your sword back into its place; for all who take the sword will perish by the sword. Do you think that I cannot appeal to my Father, and he will at once send me more than twelve legions of angels? But how then should the Scriptures be fulfilled, that it must be so?
Evangelist	At that hour Jesus said to the crowds:
Jesus	Have you come out as against a robber, with swords and clubs to capture me? Day after day I sat in the temple teaching, and you did not seize me. But all this has taken place, that the scriptures of the prophets might be fulfilled.
Evangelist	Then all the disciples forsook him and fled. Then those who had seized Jesus led him to Caiaphas the high priest, where the scribes and the elders had gathered. But Peter followed him at a distance, as far as the courtyard of the high priest, and going inside he sat with the guards to see the end. Now the chief priests and the whole council

	sought false testimony against Jesus that they might put him to death, but they found none, though many false witnesses came forward. At last two came forward:
Witnesses	This fellow said, 'I am able to destroy the temple of God, and to build it in three days'.
Evangelist	And the high priest stood up and said:
Caiaphas	Have you no answer to make? What is it that these men testify against you?
Evangelist	But Jesus was silent.
Caiaphas	I adjure you by the living God, tell us if you are the Christ, the Son of God.
Jesus	You have said so. But I tell you, hereafter you will see the Son of man seated at the right hand of Power, and coming on the clouds of heaven.
Evangelist	Then the high priest tore his robes, and said:
Caiaphas	He has uttered blasphemy. Why do we still need witnesses? You have now heard his blasphemy. What is your judgment?
Priests	He deserves death.
Evangelist	Then they spat in his face, and struck him; and some slapped him.
Priests	Prophesy to us, you Christ! Who is it that struck you?
Evangelist	Now Peter was sitting outside in the courtyard. And a maid came up to him, and said:
First Maid	You also were with Jesus the Galilean.
Evangelist	But he denied it before them all:
Peter	I do not know what you mean.
Evangelist	And when he went out to the porch, another maid saw him, and she said to the bystanders:
Second Maid	This man was with Jesus of Nazareth.
Evangelist	And again he denied it with an oath:
Peter	I do not know the man.
Evangelist	After a little while the bystanders came up and said to Peter:

Bystanders	Certainly you are also one of them, for your accent betrays you.
Evangelist	Then he began to invoke a curse on himself and to swear:
Peter	I do not know the man.
Evangelist	And immediately the cock crowed. And Peter remembered the saying of Jesus, 'Before the cock crows, you will deny me three times'. And he went out and wept bitterly. ◁ →26.75 (end)
Evangelist	27.1→ When morning came, all the chief priests and the elders of the people took counsel against Jesus to put him to death; and they bound him and led him away and delivered him to Pilate the governor. When Judas, his betrayer, saw that he was condemned, he repented and brought back the thirty pieces of silver to the chief priests and elders:
Judas	I have sinned in betraying innocent blood.
Priests	What is that to us? See to it yourself.
Evangelist	And throwing down the pieces of silver in the temple, he departed; and he went and hanged himself. But the chief priests, taking the pieces of silver, said:
Priests	It is not lawful to put them into the treasury, since they are blood money.
Evangelist	So they took counsel, and bought with them the potter's field, to bury strangers in. Therefore that field has been called the Field of Blood to this day. Then was fulfilled what had been spoken by the prophet Jeremiah, saying: 'And they took the thirty pieces of silver, the price of him on whom a price had been set by some of the sons of Israel, and they gave them for the potter's field, as the Lord directed me'. Now Jesus stood before the governor; and the governor asked him:
Pilate	Are you the King of the Jews?
Jesus	You have said so.

Evangelist	But when he was accused by the chief priests and elders, he made no answer. Then Pilate said to him:
Pilate	Do you not hear how many things they testify against you?
Evangelist	But he gave him no answer, not even to a single charge; so that the governor wondered greatly. Now at the feast the governor was accustomed to release for the crowd any one prisoner whom they wanted. And they had then a notorious prisoner, called Barabbas. So when they had gathered, Pilate said to them:
Pilate	Whom do you want me to release for you, Barabbas or Jesus who is called Christ?
Evangelist	For he knew that it was out of envy that they had delivered him up. Besides, while he was sitting on the judgment seat, his wife sent word to him:
Pilate's Wife	Have nothing to do with that righteous man, for I have suffered much over him today in a dream.
Evangelist	Now the chief priests and the elders persuaded the people to ask for Barabbas and destroy Jesus. The governor again said to them:
Pilate	Which of the two do you want me to release for you?
Crowd	Barabbas!
Pilate	Then what shall I do with Jesus who is called Christ?
Crowd	Let him be crucified.
Pilate	Why? What evil has he done?
Crowd	(louder) Let him be crucified.
Evangelist	So when Pilate saw that he was gaining nothing, but rather that a riot was beginning, he took water and washed his hands before the crowd:
Pilate	I am innocent of this man's blood; see to it yourselves.
Crowd	His blood be on us and on our children!
Evangelist	Then Pilate released for them Barabbas, and having scourged Jesus, delivered him to be crucified. Then

the soldiers of the governor took Jesus into the praetorium, and they gathered the whole battalion before him. And they stripped him and put a scarlet robe upon him, and plaiting a crown of thorns they put it on his head, and put a reed in his right hand. And kneeling before him they mocked him:

Soldiers Hail, King of the Jews!

Evangelist And they spat upon him, and took the reed and struck him on the head. And when they had mocked him, they stripped him of the robe, and put his own clothes on him, and led him away to crucify him.

As they were marching out, they came upon a man of Cyrene, Simon by name; this man they compelled to carry his cross. And when they came to a place called Golgotha (which means 'the place of a skull'), they offered him wine to drink, mingled with gall; but when he tasted it, he would not drink it. And when they had crucified him, they divided his garments among them by casting lots; then they sat down and kept watch over him there. And over his head they put the charge against him, which read, 'This is Jesus the King of the Jews'.

Then two robbers were crucified with him, one on the right and one on the left. And those who passed by derided him, wagging their heads:

Passers-by You who would destroy the Temple and build it in three days, save yourself! If you are the Son of God, come down from the cross.

Evangelist So also the chief priests, with the scribes and elders, mocked him:

Priests He saved others; he cannot save himself. He is the King of Israel; let him come down now from the cross, and we will believe in him.

He trusts in God; let God deliver him now, if he desires him; for he said: 'I am the Son of God'.

150

Evangelist	And the robbers who were crucified with him also reviled him in the same way.
	Now from the sixth hour there was darkness over all the land until the ninth hour. And about the ninth hour Jesus cried with a loud voice:
Jesus	Eli, Eli, lama sabachthani?
Evangelist	That is, 'My God, my God, why have you forsaken me?' And some of the bystanders hearing it said:
Bystanders	This man is calling Elijah.
Evangelist	And one of them at once ran and took a sponge, filled it with vinegar, put it on a reed, and gave it to him to drink. But the others said:
Bystanders	Wait; let us see whether Elijah will come to save him.
Evangelist	And Jesus cried again with a loud voice and yielded up his spirit.
	And behold, the curtain of the temple was torn in two, from top to bottom; and the earth shook, and the rocks were split; the tombs also were opened, and many bodies of the saints who had fallen asleep were raised, and coming out of the tombs after his resurrection they went into the holy city and appeared to many. When the centurion and those who were with him, keeping watch over Jesus, saw the earthquake and what took place, they were filled with awe, and said:
Centurion	Truly this was the Son of God! ◀ →27.54
Evangelist	There were also many women there, looking on from afar, who had followed Jesus from Galilee, ministering to him; among whom were Mary Magdalene, and Mary the mother of James and Joseph, and the mother of the sons of Zebedee. When it was evening, there came a rich man from Arimathea, named Joseph, who also was a disciple of Jesus. He went to Pilate and asked for the body of Jesus. Then Pilate ordered it to be given to him. And Joseph took the body, and wrapped it in a

clean linen shroud, and laid it in his own new tomb, which he had hewn in the rock; and he rolled a great stone to the door of the tomb, and departed. Mary Magdalene and the other Mary were there, sitting opposite the sepulchre. Next day, that is, after the day of Preparation, the chief priests and the Pharisees gathered before Pilate and said:

Priests Sir, we remember how that impostor said, while he was still alive, 'After three days I will rise again'. Therefore order the sepulchre to be made secure until the third day, lest his disciples go and steal him away, and tell the people, 'He has risen from the dead', and the last fraud will be worse than the first.

Pilate You have a guard of soldiers; so, make it as secure as you can.

Evangelist So they went and made the sepulchre secure by sealing the stone and setting a guard.

MARK

Mark 14 and 15

Evangelist	It was now two days before the Passover and the feast of Unleavened Bread. And the chief priests and the scribes were seeking how to arrest Jesus by stealth, and kill him; for they said:
Priests	Not during the feast, lest there be a tumult of the people.
Evangelist	And while he was at Bethany in the house of Simon the leper, as he sat at table, a woman came with an alabaster jar of ointment of pure nard, very costly; and she broke the jar and poured it over his head. But there were some who said to themselves indignantly:
Disciples	Why was the ointment thus wasted? For this ointment might have been sold for more than three hundred denarii, and given to the poor.
Evangelist	And they reproached her. But Jesus said:
Jesus	Let her alone; why do you trouble her? She has done a beautiful thing to me. For you always have the poor with you, and whenever you will, you can do good to them; but you will not always have me. She has done what she could; she has anointed my body beforehand for burying. And truly I say to you, wherever the gospel is preached in the whole world, what she has done will be told in memory of her.
Evangelist	Then Judas Iscariot, who was one of the twelve, went to the chief priests in order to betray him to them. And when they heard it, they were glad, and promised to give him money. And he sought opportunity to betray him. And on the first day of Unleavened Bread, when they sacrificed the passover lamb, his disciples said to him:

14.1→

Disciples	Where will you have us go and prepare for you to eat the passover?
Evangelist	And he sent two of his disciples and said to them:
Jesus	Go into the city, and a man carrying a jar of water will meet you; follow him, and wherever he enters, say to the householder, 'The Teacher says, "Where is my guest room, where I am to eat the passover with my disciples?"' And he will show you a large upper room furnished and ready; there prepare for us.
Evangelist	And the disciples set out and went to the city, and found it as he had told them; and they prepared the passover.
	And when it was evening he came with the twelve. And as they were at table eating, Jesus said:
Jesus	Truly, I say to you, one of you will betray me, one who is eating with me.
Evangelist	They began to be sorrowful, and to say to him one after another:
Disciples	Is it I?
Jesus	It is one of the twelve, one who is dipping bread in the same dish with me. For the Son of man goes as it is written of him, but woe to that man by whom the Son of man is betrayed! It would have been better for that man if he had not been born.
Evangelist	And as they were eating, he took bread, and blessed, and broke it, and gave it to them, and said:
Jesus	Take; this is my body.
Evangelist	And he took a cup, and when he had given thanks he gave it to them, and they all drank of it.
Jesus	This is my blood of the covenant, which is poured out for many. Truly, I say to you, I shall not drink again of the fruit of the vine until that day when I drink it new in the kingdom of God.
Evangelist	▷ And when they had sung a hymn, they went out to the Mount of Olives. And Jesus said to them:
Jesus	You will all fall away; for it is written, 'I will strike

14.2

	the shepherd, and the sheep will be scattered'. But after I am raised up, I will go before you to Galilee.
Evangelist	Peter said to him:
Peter	Even though they all fall away, I will not.
Jesus	Truly, I say to you, this very night, before the cock crows twice, you will deny me three times.
Peter	(*vehemently*) If I must die with you, I will not deny you.
Evangelist	And they all said the same.
	▶ And they went to a place called Gethsemane; and he said to his disciples:
Jesus	Sit here, while I pray.
Evangelist	And he took with him Peter and James and John, and began to be greatly distressed and troubled. And he said to them:
Jesus	My soul is very sorrowful, even to death; remain here, and watch.
Evangelist	And going a little farther, he fell on the ground and prayed that, if it were possible, the hour might pass from him:
Jesus	Abba, Father, all things are possible to you; remove this cup from me; yet not what I will, but what you will.
Evangelist	And he came and found them sleeping, and he said to Peter:
Jesus	Simon, are you asleep? Could you not watch one hour? Watch and pray that you may not enter into temptation; the spirit indeed is willing, but the flesh is weak.
Evangelist	And again he went away and prayed, saying the same words. And again he came and found them sleeping, for their eyes were very heavy; and they did not know what to answer him. And he came the third time, and said to them:
Jesus	Are you still sleeping and taking your rest? It is enough; the hour has come; the Son of man is

→14.31

14.32→

155

	betrayed into the hands of sinners. Rise, let us be going; see, my betrayer is at hand.
Evangelist	And immediately, while he was still speaking, Judas came, one of the twelve, and with him a crowd with swords and clubs, from the chief priests and the scribes and the elders. Now the betrayer had given them a sign:
Judas	The one I shall kiss is the man; seize him and lead him away safely.
Evangelist	And when he came, he went up to him at once, and said:
Judas	Master!
Evangelist	And he kissed him. And they laid hands on him and seized him. But one of those who stood by drew his sword, and struck the slave of the high priest and cut off his ear. And Jesus said to them:
Jesus	Have you come out as against a robber, with swords and clubs to capture me? Day after day I was with you in the Temple teaching, and you did not seize me. But let the Scriptures be fulfilled.
Evangelist	And they all forsook him and fled. And a young man followed him, with nothing but a linen cloth about his body; and they seized him, but he left the linen cloth and ran away naked.
	And they led Jesus to the high priest; and all the chief priests and the scribes and the elders were assembled. And Peter had followed him at a distance, right into the courtyard of the high priest; and he was sitting with the guards, and warming himself at the fire.
	Now the chief priests and the whole council sought testimony against Jesus to put him to death; but they found none. For many bore false witness against him, and their witness did not agree. And some stood up and bore false witness against him:
Witnesses	We heard him say, 'I will destroy this temple that is made with hands, and in three days I will build another, not made with hands'.

Evangelist	Yet not even so did their testimony agree. And the high priest stood up in the midst, and asked Jesus:
High Priest	Have you no answer to make? What is it that these men testify against you?
Evangelist	But he was silent and made no answer. Again the high priest asked him:
High Priest	Are you the Christ, the Son of the Blessed?
Jesus	I am; and you will see the Son of man sitting at the right hand of Power, and coming with the clouds of heaven.
Evangelist	And the high priest tore his mantle, and said:
High Priest	Why do we still need witnesses? You have heard his blasphemy. What is your decision?
Evangelist	And they all condemned him as deserving death. And some began to spit on him, and to cover his face, and to strike him, saying to him:
Scribes	Prophesy!
Evangelist	And the guards received him with blows. And as Peter was below in the courtyard, one of the maids of the high priest came; and seeing Peter warming himself, she looked at him, and said:
Maid	You also were with the Nazarene, Jesus.
Evangelist	But he denied it:
Peter	I neither know nor understand what you mean.
Evangelist	And he went out into the gateway. And the maid saw him, and began again to say to the bystanders:
Maid	This man is one of them.
Evangelist	But again he denied it. And after a little while again the bystanders said to Peter:
Bystanders	Certainly you are one of them; for you are a Galilean.
Evangelist	But he began to invoke a curse on himself and to swear:
Peter	I do not know this man of whom you speak.
Evangelist	And immediately the cock crowed a second time. And Peter remembered how Jesus had said to him, 'Before the cock crows twice, you will deny me three times'. And he broke down and wept. ◁ →14.72 (end)

157

And as soon as it was morning the chief priests, 15.1→
with the elders and scribes, and the whole council
held a consultation; and they bound Jesus and led
him away and delivered him to Pilate, and Pilate
asked him:

Pilate Are you the King of the Jews?

Jesus You have said so.

Evangelist And the chief priests accused him of many things.
And Pilate again asked him:

Pilate Have you no answer to make? See how many
charges they bring against you.

Evangelist But Jesus made no further answer, so that Pilate
wondered. Now at the feast he used to release for
them any one prisoner for whom they asked. And
among the rebels in prison, who had committed
murder in the insurrection, there was a man called
Barabbas. And the crowd came up and began to ask
Pilate to do as he was wont to do for them. And he
answered them:

Pilate Do you want me to release for you the King of the
Jews?

Evangelist For he perceived that it was out of envy that the
chief priests had delivered him up. But the chief
priests stirred up the crowd to have him release for
them Barabbas instead. And Pilate again said to
them:

Pilate Then what shall I do with the man whom you call
the King of the Jews?

Crowd Crucify him, crucify him.

Pilate Why? What evil has he done?

Crowd (*louder*) Crucify him, crucify him.

Evangelist So Pilate, wishing to satisfy the crowd, released for
them Barabbas; and having scourged Jesus, he
delivered him to be crucified.
And the soldiers led him away inside the palace
(that is, the praetorium); and they called together
the whole battalion. And they clothed him in a

purple cloak, and plaiting a crown of thorns they put it on him. And they began to salute him:

Soldiers Hail, King of the Jews!

Evangelist And they struck his head with a reed, and spat upon him, and they knelt down in homage to him. And when they had mocked him, they stripped him of the purple cloak, and put his own clothes on him. And they led him out to crucify him. And they compelled a passer-by, Simon of Cyrene, who was coming in from the country, the father of Alexander and Rufus, to carry his cross. And they brought him to Golgotha (which means 'the place of a skull'). And they offered him wine mingled with myrrh; but he did not take it. And they crucified him, and divided his garments among them, casting lots for them, to decide what each should take. And it was the third hour, when they crucified him. And the inscription of the charge against him read, 'The King of the Jews'. And with him they crucified two robbers, one on his right and one on his left. And those who passed by derided him, wagging their heads:

Passers-by Aha! You who would destroy the temple and build it in three days, save yourself, and come down from the cross!

Evangelist So also the chief priests mocked him to one another with the scribes:

Priests He saved others; he cannot save himself. Let the Christ, the King of Israel, come down now from the cross, that we may see and believe.

Evangelist Those who were crucified with him also reviled him.

And when the sixth hour had come, there was darkness over the whole land until the ninth hour. And at the ninth hour Jesus cried with a loud voice:

Jesus Eloï, Eloï, lama sabachthani?

Evangelist Which means, 'My God, my God, why have you

159

	forsaken me?' And some of the bystanders hearing it said:
Bystanders	Behold, he is calling Elijah.
Evangelist	And one ran and, filling a sponge full of vinegar, put it on a reed and gave it to him to drink:
Bystander	Wait; let us see whether Elijah will come to take him down.
Evangelist	And Jesus uttered a loud cry, and breathed his last. And the curtain of the Temple was torn in two, from top to bottom. And when the centurion, who stood facing him, saw that he thus breathed his last, he said:
Centurion	Truly this man was the Son of God! ◄
Evangelist	There were also women looking on from afar, among whom were Mary Magdalene, and Mary the mother of James the younger and of Joses, and Salome, who when he was in Galilee, followed him, and ministered to him; and also many other women who came up with him to Jerusalem. And when evening had come, since it was the day of Preparation, that is, the day before the sabbath, Joseph of Arimathea, a respected member of the council, who was also himself looking for the kingdom of God, took courage and went to Pilate, and asked for the body of Jesus. And Pilate wondered if he were already dead; and summoning the centurion, he asked him whether he was already dead. And when he learned from the centurion that he was dead, he granted the body to Joseph. And he bought a linen shroud, and taking him down, wrapped him in the linen shroud, and laid him in a tomb which had been hewn out of the rock; and he rolled a stone against the door of the tomb. Mary Magdalene and Mary the mother of Joses saw where he was laid.

→15

LUKE

Luke 22 and 23

Evangelist	Now the feast of Unleavened Bread drew near, 22.1→ which is called the Passover. And the chief priests and the scribes were seeking how to put Jesus to death; for they feared the people. Then Satan entered into Judas called Iscariot, who was of the number of the twelve; he went away and conferred with the chief priests and captains how he might betray him to them. And they were glad and engaged to give him money. So he agreed, and sought an opportunity to betray him to them in the absence of the multitude. Then came the day of Unleavened Bread, on which the passover lamb had to be sacrificed. So Jesus sent Peter and John, saying:
Jesus	Go and prepare the passover for us, that we may eat it.
Peter	Where will you have us prepare it?
Jesus	Behold, when you have entered the city, a man carrying a jar of water will meet you; follow him into the house which he enters, and tell the householder, 'The Teacher says to you, "Where is the guest room, where I am to eat the passover with my disciples?"' And he will show you a large upper room furnished; there make ready.
Evangelist	And they went, and found it as he had told them; and they prepared the passover. And when the hour came, he sat at table, and the apostles with him. And he said to them:
Jesus	I have earnestly desired to eat this passover with you before I suffer; for I tell you I shall not eat it until it is fulfilled in the kingdom of God.

Evangelist	And he took a cup, and when he had given thanks he said:
Jesus	Take this, and divide it among yourselves; for I tell you that from now on I shall not drink of the fruit of the vine until the kingdom of God comes.
Evangelist	And he took bread, and when he had given thanks he broke it and gave it to them, saying:
Jesus	This is my body. But behold, the hand of him who betrays me is with me on the table. For the Son of man goes as it has been determined; but woe to that man by whom he is betrayed.
Evangelist	And they began to question one another, which of them it was that would do this. A dispute also arose among them, which of them was to be regarded as the greatest.
Jesus	The kings of the Gentiles exercise lordship over them, and those in authority over them are called benefactors. But not so with you; rather let the greatest among you become as the youngest, and the leader as one who serves. For which is the greater, one who sits at table, or one who serves? Is it not the one who sits at table? But I am among you as one who serves. You are those who have continued with me in my trials; as my Father appointed a kingdom for me, so do I appoint for you that you may eat and drink at my table in my kingdom, and sit on thrones judging the twelve tribes of Israel.
Evangelist	▷ Jesus said to Simon Peter:
Jesus	Simon, Simon, behold, Satan demanded to have you, that he might sift you like wheat, but I have prayed for you that your faith may not fail; and when you have turned again, strengthen your brethren.
Peter	Lord, I am ready to go with you to prison and to death.
Jesus	I tell you, Peter, the cock will not crow this day, until you three times deny that you know me.

22.31

	When I sent you out with no purse or bag or sandals, did you lack anything?
Disciples	Nothing.
Jesus	But now, let him who has a purse take it, and likewise a bag. And let him who has no sword sell his mantle and buy one. For I tell you that this scripture must be fulfilled in me, 'And he was reckoned with transgressors'; for what is written about me has its fulfilment.
Disciples	Look, Lord, here are two swords.
Jesus	It is enough.
Evangelist	▶ And he came out, and went, as was his custom, to the Mount of Olives; and the disciples followed him. And when he came to the place he said:
Jesus	Pray that you may not enter into temptation.
Evangelist	And he withdrew from them about a stone's throw, and knelt down and prayed:
Jesus	Father, if you are willing, remove this cup from me; nevertheless not my will, but yours, be done.
Evangelist	And there appeared to him an angel from heaven, strengthening him. And being in an agony he prayed more earnestly; and his sweat became like great drops of blood falling down upon the ground. And when he rose from prayer, he came to the disciples and found them sleeping for sorrow, and he said to them:
Jesus	Why do you sleep? Rise and pray that you may not enter into temptation.
Evangelist	While he was still speaking, there came a crowd, and the man called Judas, one of the twelve, was leading them. He drew near to Jesus to kiss him; but Jesus said to him:
Jesus	Judas, would you betray the Son of man with a kiss?
Evangelist	And when those who were about him saw what would follow, they said:
Disciples	Lord, shall we strike with the sword?

→22.38

22.39→

Evangelist	And one of them struck the slave of the high priest and cut off his right ear. But Jesus said:
Jesus	No more of this!
Evangelist	And he touched his ear and healed him. Then Jesus said to the chief priests and captains of the Temple and elders who had come out against him:
Jesus	Have you come out as against a robber, with swords and clubs? When I was with you day after day in the Temple, you did not lay hands on me. But this is your hour, and the power of darkness.
Evangelist	Then they seized him and led him away, bringing him into the high priest's house. Peter followed at a distance; and when they had kindled a fire in the middle of the courtyard and sat down together, Peter sat among them. Then a maid, seeing him as he sat in the light and gazing at him, said:
Maid	This man also was with him.
Evangelist	But he denied it:
Peter	Woman, I do not know him.
Evangelist	And a little later some one else saw him and said:
Bystander 1	You also are one of them.
Peter	Man, I am not.
Evangelist	And after an interval of about an hour, still another insisted:
Bystander 2	Certainly this man also was with him; for he is a Galilean.
Peter	Man, I do not know what you are saying.
Evangelist	And immediately, while he was still speaking, the cock crowed. And the Lord turned and looked at Peter. And Peter remembered the word of the Lord, how he had said to him, 'Before the cock crows today, you will deny me three times'. And he went out and wept bitterly. ◁ →22
	Now the men who were holding Jesus mocked him and beat him; they also blindfolded him and asked him:
Men	Prophesy! Who is it that struck you?

Evangelist	And they spoke many other words against him, reviling him.
Evangelist	When day came, the assembly of the elders of the people gathered together, both chief priests and scribes; and they led him away to their council, and they said:
Priests	If you are the Christ, tell us.
Jesus	If I tell you, you will not believe; and if I ask you, you will not answer. But from now on the Son of man shall be seated at the right hand of the power of God.
Priests	Are you the Son of God, then?
Jesus	You say that I am.
Priests	What further testimony do we need? We have heard it ourselves from his own lips.
Evangelist	Then the whole company of them arose, and brought him before Pilate. And they began to accuse him:
Priests	We found this man perverting our nation, and forbidding us to give tribute to Caesar, and saying that he himself is Christ a king.
Pilate	Are you the King of the Jews?
Jesus	You have said so.
Pilate	(to the priests) I find no crime in this man.
Priests	(urgently) He stirs up the people, teaching throughout all Judea, from Galilee even to this place.
Evangelist	When Pilate heard this, he asked whether the man was a Galilean. And when he learned that he belonged to Herod's jurisdiction, he sent him over to Herod, who was himself in Jerusalem at that time. When Herod saw Jesus, he was very glad, for he had long desired to see him, because he had heard about him, and he was hoping to see some sign done by him. So he questioned him at length, but Jesus made no answer. The chief priests and the scribes stood by, vehemently accusing him. And

→22.65
22.66→

Herod with his soldiers treated him with contempt and mocked him; then, arraying him in gorgeous apparel, he sent him back to Pilate.

And Herod and Pilate became friends with each other that very day, for before this they had been at enmity with each other.

Pilate then called together the chief priests and the rulers and the people, and said to them:

Pilate You brought me this man as one who was perverting the people; and after examining him before you, behold, I did not find this man guilty of any of your charges against him; neither did Herod, for he sent him back to us. Behold, nothing deserving death has been done by him; I will therefore chastise him and release him.

Evangelist But they all cried out together:

Priests Away with this man, and release to us Barabbas.

Evangelist A man who had been thrown into prison for an insurrection started in the city, and for murder. Pilate addressed them once more, desiring to release Jesus; but they shouted out:

Priests Crucify him, crucify him!

Evangelist A third time he spoke to them:

Pilate Why? What evil has he done? I have found in him no crime deserving death; I will therefore chastise him and release him.

Evangelist But they were urgent, demanding with loud cries that he should be crucified. And their voices prevailed. So Pilate gave sentence that their demand should be granted. He released the man who had been thrown into prison for insurrection and murder, whom they asked for; but Jesus he delivered up to their will.

And as they led him away, they seized one Simon of Cyrene, who was coming in from the country, and laid on him the cross, to carry it behind Jesus. And there followed him a great multitude of the

	people, and of women who bewailed and lamented him. But Jesus turning to them said:
Jesus	Daughters of Jerusalem, do not weep for me, but weep for yourselves and for your children. For behold, the days are coming when they will say, 'Blessed are the barren, and the wombs that never bore, and the breasts that never gave suck!' Then they will begin to say to the mountains, 'Fall on us'; and to the hills, 'Cover us'. For if they do this when the wood is green, what will happen when it is dry?
Evangelist	Two others also, who were criminals, were led away to be put to death with him. And when they came to the place which is called The Skull, there they crucified him, and the criminals, one on the right and one on the left. And Jesus said:
Jesus	Father, forgive them; for they know not what they do.
Evangelist	And they cast lots to divide his garments. And the people stood by, watching; but the rulers scoffed at him:
Priests	He saved others; let him save himself, if he is the Christ of God, his Chosen One!
Evangelist	The soldiers also mocked him, coming up and offering him vinegar:
Soldiers	If you are the King of the Jews, save yourself!
Evangelist	There was also an inscription over him, 'This is the King of the Jews'. One of the criminals who were hanged railed at him:
Robber 1	Are you not the Christ? Save yourself and us!
Evangelist	But the other rebuked him:
Robber 2	Do you not fear God, since you are under the same sentence of condemnation? And we indeed justly; for we are receiving the due reward of our deeds; but this man has done nothing wrong. Jesus, remember me when you come in your kingly power.

Jesus	Truly, I say to you, today you will be with me in Paradise.
Evangelist	It was now about the sixth hour, and there was darkness over the whole land until the ninth hour, while the sun's light failed; and the curtain of the Temple was torn in two. Then Jesus cried with a loud voice:
Jesus	Father, into your hands I commit my spirit.
Evangelist	And having said this he breathed his last. Now when the centurion saw what had taken place, he praised God:
Centurion	Certainly this man was innocent!
Evangelist	And all the multitudes who assembled to see the sight, when they saw what had taken place, returned home beating their breasts. ◀ →23. And all his acquaintances and the women who had followed him from Galilee stood at a distance and saw these things.

Now there was a man named Joseph from the Jewish town of Arimathea. He was a member of the council, a good and righteous man, who had not consented to their purpose and deed, and he was looking for the kingdom of God. This man went to Pilate and asked for the body of Jesus. Then he took it down and wrapped it in a linen shroud, and laid him in a rock-hewn tomb, where no one had ever yet been laid. It was the day of Preparation, and the sabbath was beginning. The women who had come with him from Galilee followed, and saw the tomb, and how his body was laid; then they returned, and prepared spices and ointments. On the sabbath they rested according to the commandment.

JOHN

John 18 and 19

Evangelist	When Jesus had spoken these words, he went forth with his disciples across the Kidron valley, where there was a garden which he and his disciples entered. Now Judas, who betrayed him, also knew the place; for Jesus often met there with his disciples. So Judas, procuring a band of soldiers and some officers from the chief priests and the Pharisees, went there with lanterns and torches and weapons. Then Jesus, knowing all that was to befall him, came forward and said to them:
Jesus	Whom do you seek?
Soldiers	Jesus of Nazareth.
Jesus	I am he.
Evangelist	Judas, who betrayed him, was standing with them. When he said to them, 'I am he', they drew back and fell to the ground. Again he asked them:
Jesus	Whom do you seek?
Soldiers	Jesus of Nazareth.
Jesus	I told you that I am he; so, if you seek me, let these men go.
Evangelist	This was to fulfil the word which he had spoken, 'Of those whom you gave me I lost not one'. Then Simon Peter, having a sword, drew it and struck the high priest's slave and cut off his right ear. The slave's name was Malchus. Jesus said to Peter:
Jesus	Put your sword into its sheath; shall I not drink the cup which the Father has given me?
Evangelist	So the band of soldiers and their captain and the officers of the Jews seized Jesus and bound him. First they led him to Annas; for he was the father-in-law of Caiaphas, who was high priest that year. It was Caiaphas who had given counsel to the Jews that it was expedient that one man should die for

18.1→

the people. Simon Peter followed Jesus, and so did another disciple. As this disciple was known to the high priest, he entered the court of the high priest along with Jesus, while Peter stood outside at the door. So the other disciple, who was known to the high priest, went out and spoke to the maid who kept the door, and brought Peter in. The maid who kept the door said to Peter:

Maid	Are you not also one of this man's disciples?
Peter	I am not.
Evangelist	Now the servants and officers had made a charcoal fire, because it was cold, and they were standing and warming themselves; Peter also was with them, standing and warming himself. The high priest then questioned Jesus about his disciples and his teaching. Jesus answered:
Jesus	I have spoken openly to the world; I have always taught in synagogues and in the temple, where all Jews come together; I have said nothing secretly. Why do you ask me? Ask those who have heard me, what I said to them; they know what I said.
Evangelist	When he had said this, one of the officers standing by struck Jesus with his hand, saying:
Officer	Is that how you answer the high priest?
Jesus	If I have spoken wrongly, bear witness to the wrong; but if I have spoken rightly, why do you strike me?
Evangelist	Annas then sent him bound to Caiaphas the high priest. Now Simon Peter was standing and warming himself. They said to him:
Bystanders	Are you not also one of his disciples?
Peter	I am not.
Evangelist	One of the servants of the high priest, a kinsman of the man whose ear Peter had cut off, said:
Servant	Did I not see you in the garden with him?
Evangelist	Peter again denied it; and at once the cock crowed. Then they led Jesus from the house of Caiaphas to

the praetorium. It was early. They themselves did not enter the praetorium, so that they might not be defiled, but might eat the passover. So Pilate went out to them and said:

Pilate	What accusation do you bring against this man?
Priests	If this man were not an evildoer, we would not have handed him over.
Pilate	Take him yourselves and judge him by your own law.
Priests	It is not lawful for us to put any man to death.
Evangelist	This was to fulfil the word which Jesus had spoken to show by what death he was to die. Pilate entered the praetorium again and called Jesus and said to him:
Pilate	Are you the King of the Jews?
Jesus	Do you say this of your own accord, or did others say it to you about me?
Pilate	Am I a Jew? Your own nation and the chief priests have handed you over to me; what have you done?
Jesus	My kingship is not of this world; if my kingship were of this world, my servants would fight, that I might not be handed over to the Jews; but my kingship is not from the world.
Pilate	So you are a king?
Jesus	You say that I am a king. For this I was born, and for this I have come into the world, to bear witness to the truth. Every one who is of the truth hears my voice.
Pilate	What is truth?
Evangelist	After he had said this, he went out to the Jews again, and told them:
Pilate	I find no crime in him. But you have a custom that I should release one man for you at the Passover; will you have me release for you the King of the Jews?
Priests	Not this man, but Barabbas!
Evangelist	Now Barabbas was a robber.

Then Pilate took Jesus and scourged him. And the

soldiers plaited a crown of thorns, and put it on his head, and arrayed him in a purple robe; they came up to him, saying:

Soldiers	Hail, King of the Jews!
Evangelist	Pilate went out again, and said to the Jews:
Pilate	Behold, I am bringing him out to you, that you may know that I find no crime in him.
Evangelist	So Jesus came out, wearing the crown of thorns and the purple robe.
Pilate	Here is the man!
Evangelist	When the chief priests and the officers saw him, they cried out:
Priests	Crucify him! Crucify him!
Pilate	Take him yourselves and crucify him, for I find no crime in him.
Priests	We have a law, and by that law he ought to die, because he has made himself the Son of God.
Evangelist	When Pilate heard these words, he was the more afraid; he entered the praetorium again and said to Jesus:
Pilate	Where are you from?
Evangelist	But Jesus gave no answer.
Pilate	You will not speak to me? Do you not know that I have power to release you, and power to crucify you?
Jesus	You would have no power over me unless it had been given you from above; therefore he who delivered me to you has the greater sin.
Evangelist	Upon this Pilate sought to release him, but the Jews cried out:
Priests	If you release this man, you are not Caesar's friend; every one who makes himself a king sets himself against Caesar.
Evangelist	When Pilate heard these words, he brought Jesus out and sat down on the judgment seat at a place called The Pavement, and in Hebrew, Gabbatha. Now it was the day of Preparation for the Passover;

	it was about the sixth hour. He said to the Jews:
Pilate	Here is your King!
Priests	Away with him, away with him, crucify him!
Pilate	Shall I crucify your King?
Priests	We have no king but Caesar.
Evangelist	Then he handed Jesus over to them to be crucified. So they took Jesus, and he went out, bearing his own cross, to the place called The Skull, which is called in Hebrew Golgotha. There they crucified him, and with him two others, one on either side, and Jesus between them. Pilate also wrote a title and put it on the cross; it read, 'Jesus of Nazareth, the King of the Jews'. Many of the Jews read this title, for the place where Jesus was crucified was near the city; and it was written in Hebrew, in Latin, and in Greek. The chief priests of the Jews then said to Pilate:
Priests	Do not write, 'The King of the Jews', but, 'This man said, "I am the King of the Jews"'.
Pilate	What I have written, I have written.
Evangelist	When the soldiers had crucified Jesus they took his garments and made four parts, one for each soldier. But his tunic was without seam, woven from top to bottom; so they said to one another:
Soldiers	Let us not tear it, but cast lots for it to see whose it shall be.
Evangelist	This was to fulfil the scripture, 'They parted my garments among them, and for my clothing they cast lots'. So the soldiers did this. Standing by the cross of Jesus were his mother, and his mother's sister, Mary the wife of Clopas, and Mary Magdalene. When Jesus saw his mother, and the disciple whom he loved standing near, he said to his mother:
Jesus	Woman, behold your son.
Evangelist	Then he said to the disciple:
Jesus	Behold your mother.

173

Evangelist	And from that hour the disciple took her to his own home.
	After this Jesus, knowing that all was now finished, said (to fulfil the scripture):
Jesus	I thirst.
Evangelist	A bowl full of vinegar stood there; so they put a sponge full of the vinegar on hyssop and held it to his mouth. When Jesus had received the vinegar, he said:
Jesus	It is finished.
Evangelist	And he bowed his head and gave up his spirit.

Since it was the day of Preparation, in order to prevent the bodies from remaining on the cross on the sabbath (for that sabbath was a high day), the Jews asked Pilate that their legs might be broken, and that they might be taken away. So the soldiers came and broke the legs of the first, and of the other who had been crucified with him; but when they came to Jesus and saw that he was already dead, they did not break his legs. But one of the soldiers pierced his side with a spear, and at once there came out blood and water. He who saw it has borne witness – his testimony is true, and he knows that he tells the truth – that you also may believe. For these things took place that the scripture might be fulfilled, 'Not a bone of him shall be broken'. And again another scripture says, 'They shall look on him whom they have pierced.'

→19.3

After this Joseph of Arimathea, who was a disciple of Jesus, but secretly, for fear of the Jews, asked Pilate that he might take away the body of Jesus, and Pilate gave him leave. So he came and took away his body. Nicodemus also, who had at first come to him by night, came bringing a mixture of myrrh and aloes, about a hundred pounds' weight. They took the body of Jesus, and bound it in linen cloths with the spices, as is the burial custom of the

Jews. Now in the place where he was crucified there was a garden, and in the garden a new tomb where no one had ever been laid. So because of the Jewish day of Preparation, as the tomb was close at hand, they laid Jesus there.

MAUNDY THURSDAY AND GOOD FRIDAY

MAUNDY THURSDAY AND GOOD FRIDAY

MAUNDY THURSDAY

INTRODUCTION

Maundy Thursday marks a new beginning, the beginning of the end. From this point on, our Christian worship is a continuum through to Easter morning. The Jewish beginning of the day (in the evening) unites the events of Maundy Thursday with the death of Christ the next afternoon. The provision that the services may continue into a Watch underlines this continuity. The Watch should be observed at least for an hour, preferably until midnight, if not until the liturgy of Good Friday.

Because this service is part of the continuous observance in the parish church of the last events of Jesus' life, there is no provision here for the blessing of oils, for which provision is made in the ASB pp. 555–557.

The service is so designed that there are different possible emphases to be discerned within it. First, it is possible to stress the theme of love and service, as the Gospel suggests. This theme, echoing also the reconciliation of penitents, begins with the opening sentence, continues with the emphasis on love and cleansing in the sentences and invitation to confession, and with the choice of the confession containing the phrase 'wounded your love', and is demonstrated in the washing of feet. It is this action which gives us the derivation of the word Maundy, from the first words of the traditional anthem 'Mandatum novum do vobis' ('A new commandment I give you', John 13.34).

Second, it is possible to stress the institution of the Lord's Supper, as the Epistle suggests. This carries with it the theme of

179

redemption and so makes the eucharist a prefiguring of the eucharist on Easter Day, as suggested by the collect, the reading from Exodus 12, and the psalms.

NOTES

1   **The Prayers of Penitence**   These may be omitted if the washing of feet is observed and section 3 and the prayer no. 13 of Prayers on the Passion (p. 94) may be used instead of the prayer at section 16.

2   **The Washing of Feet**   Where this is customary, up to twelve chairs may be conveniently placed. After the sermon, those taking part move to their places. The president, with a basin of water and a towel, kneels before each, pours water over the uncovered foot and touches it with the towel. Another towel should be available for complete drying.

3   **Anthems at the Washing of Feet**   The hymn 'Ubi caritas' ('God is love, and where true love is', 'Where love and loving-kindness dwell') is particularly suitable at this point, as is Psalm 40.

4   **The Agape**   Where this is desired, the order on p. 98 may be used.

5   **The Words of Institution**   In the Eucharistic Prayer on Maundy Thursday evening the president may substitute for the words 'who in the same night that he was betrayed' the words 'who in this night when he was betrayed'.

6   **The Watch**   If the Watch is to be kept the Dismissal is omitted. The coverings may be removed from the holy table and the lights extinguished during or immediately after the Gospel of the Watch or the reading of John 17 or during a hymn or psalm. If the Watch is kept in a different part of the church there may be a procession accompanied by the singing of a hymn or a psalm.

7   **Holy Communion**   If it is intended that the people should complete their observance by receiving Holy Communion on Good Friday, the sacrament should be kept in a safe and seemly place.

8   **Liturgical Colour**   White or gold. If for this service it is the custom for crosses etc. to be covered, they should be veiled in plain white linen.

MAUNDY THURSDAY

THE PREPARATION

1   At the entrance of the ministers THIS SENTENCE may be used.

> A new commandment I give to you, that you love one another, as I have loved you. *John 13.34*

and A HYMN, A CANTICLE, or A PSALM may be sung.

▶ 2   The president welcomes the people using these or other appropriate words.

> The grace of our Lord Jesus Christ, and the love of God, and the fellowship of the Holy Spirit be with you all

All   **and also with you.**

PRAYERS OF PENITENCE

3   The minister may say these sentences.

> Our Lord Jesus Christ says
> If you love me, keep my commandments.
> *John 14.15*
> Unless I wash you, you have no part with me.
> *John 13.8*

▶ 4   Minister   Let us confess to almighty God our sins against his love, and ask him to cleanse us.

▶ 5   **All**   **Father eternal, giver of light and grace,**
> **we have sinned against you and against our**
>   **neighbour,**
> **in what we have thought,**
> **in what we have said and done,**
> **through ignorance, through weakness,**

through our own deliberate fault.
We have wounded your love,
and marred your image in us.
We are sorry and ashamed,
and repent of all our sins.
For the sake of your Son Jesus Christ, who
    died for us,
forgive us all that is past;
and lead us out from darkness
to walk as children of light.   Amen.

► 6   President   Almighty God,
who forgives all who truly repent,
have mercy upon *you*,
pardon and deliver *you* from all *your* sins,
confirm and strengthen *you* in all goodness,
and keep *you* in life eternal;
through Jesus Christ our Lord.   **Amen.**

7   KYRIE ELEISON or THE TRISAGION may be said
(see pp. 285–286).

► 8   **All**   **Glory to God in the highest
and peace to his people on earth.**

**Lord God, heavenly King,
almighty God and Father,
we worship you, we give you thanks,
we praise you for your glory.**

**Lord Jesus Christ, only Son of the Father,
Lord God, Lamb of God,
you take away the sin of the world:
have mercy on us;
you are seated at the right hand of the
    Father:
receive our prayer.**

**For you alone are the Holy One,
you alone are the Lord,**

**you alone are the Most High,
Jesus Christ,
with the Holy Spirit,
in the glory of God the Father.   Amen.**

▶ 9   The president says THE COLLECT.

God our Father,
you have invited us to share in the supper
which your Son gave to his Church
to proclaim his death until he comes.
May he nourish us by his presence,
and unite us in his love;
who is alive and reigns with you and the
    Holy Spirit,
one God now and for ever.   **Amen.**

THE MINISTRY OF THE WORD

10   **Sit**
OLD TESTAMENT READING

Exodus 12.1-8, 11-14 NEB

The Lord said to Moses and Aaron in Egypt: This month is
for you the first of months; you shall make it the first month
of the year. Speak to the whole community of Israel and say
to them: On the tenth day of this month let each man take a
lamb or a kid for his family, one for each household, but if a
household is too small for one lamb or one kid, then the man
and his nearest neighbour may take one between them. They
shall share the cost, taking into account both the number of
persons and the amount each of them eats. Your lamb or kid
must be without blemish, a yearling male. You may take
equally a sheep or a goat. You must have it in safe keeping
until the fourteenth day of this month, and then all the
assembled community of Israel shall slaughter the victim

between dusk and dark. They must take some of the blood and smear it on the two door-posts and on the lintel of every house in which they eat the lamb. On that night they shall eat the flesh roast on the fire; they shall eat it with unleavened cakes and bitter herbs.

This is the way in which you must eat it: you shall have your belt fastened, your sandals on your feet and your staff in your hand, and you must eat in urgent haste. It is the Lord's Passover. On that night I shall pass through the land of Egypt and kill every first-born of man and beast. Thus will I execute judgement, I the Lord, against all the gods of Egypt. And as for you, the blood will be a sign on the houses in which you are: when I see the blood I will pass over you; the mortal blow shall not touch you, when I strike the land of Egypt.

You shall keep this day as a day of remembrance, and make it a pilgrim-feast, a festival of the Lord; you shall keep it generation after generation as a rule for all time.

At the end the reader may say

This is the word of the Lord.

All   **Thanks be to God.**

▶ 11   *Psalm 116.11-end*

This response may be used.

**The cup of blessing which we bless,
is it not a sharing of the blood of Christ?**

11 How shall I re|pay the | Lord:
    for | all his | bene·fits | to me?

12 I will take up the | cup of · sal|vation:
    and | call up·on the | name · of the | Lord.   **R**

13 I will pay my ˈ vows · to the ˈ Lord:
    in the ˈ presence · of ˈ all his ˈ people.

14 Grievous in the ˈ sight · of the ˈ Lord:
    is the ˈ death ˈ of his ˈ faithful ones.   **R**

15 O Lord I am your servant
    your servant and the ˈ son of · your ˈ handmaid:
    you ˈ have un ˈ loosed my ˈ bonds.

16 I will offer you a sacrifice of ˈ thanks ˈ giving:
    and ˈ call up · on the ˈ name · of the ˈ Lord.   **R**

17 I will pay my ˈ vows · to the ˈ Lord:
    In the ˈ presence · of ˈ all his ˈ people,

18 In the courts of the ˈ house · of the ˈ Lord:
    even in your midst O Jerusalem ˈ
      Praise ˈ – the ˈ Lord.   **R**

12 NEW TESTAMENT READING (EPISTLE)

1 Corinthians 11.23-29 NEB

The tradition which I handed on to you came to me from the
Lord himself: that the Lord Jesus, on the night of his arrest,
took bread and, after giving thanks to God, broke it and said:
'This is my body, which is for you; do this as a memorial of
me.' In the same way, he took the cup after supper, and said:
This cup is the new covenant sealed by my blood. Whenever
you drink it, do this as a memorial of me.' For every time
you eat this bread and drink the cup, you proclaim the death
of the Lord, until he comes.

It follows that anyone who eats the bread or drinks the cup of
the Lord unworthily will be guilty of desecrating the body
and blood of the Lord. A man must test himself before eating
his share of the bread and drinking from the cup. For he who

eats and drinks eats and drinks judgement on himself if he does not discern the Body.

At the end the reader may say

This is the word of the Lord.

All   **Thanks be to God.**

13   THIS ANTHEM, or A HYMN, or A CANTICLE may be sung.

A new commandment I give unto you:
that you love one another as I have loved you.
By this shall all men know that you are my
     disciples
if you have love for one another.

▶ 14   **Stand**
THE GOSPEL

When it is announced

All   **Glory to Christ our Saviour.**

John 13.1-15 NEB

It was before the Passover festival. Jesus knew that his hour had come and he must leave this world and go to the Father. He had always loved his own who were in the world, and now he was to show the full extent of his love.

The devil had already put it into the mind of Judas son of Simon Iscariot to betray him. During supper Jesus, well aware that the Father had entrusted everything to him, and that he had come from God and was going back to God, rose from table, laid aside his garments, and taking a towel, tied it round him. Then he poured water into a basin, and began to wash his disciples' feet and to wipe them with the towel.

When it was Simon Peter's turn, Peter said to him, 'You, Lord, washing my feet?' Jesus replied, 'You do not understand now what I am doing, but one day you will.' Peter said, 'I will never let you wash my feet.' 'If I do not wash you,' Jesus replied, 'you are not in fellowship with me.'

'Then Lord,' said Simon Peter, 'not my feet only; wash my hands and head as well!'

Jesus said, 'A man who has bathed needs no further washing; he is altogether clean; and you are clean, though not every one of you.' He added the words, 'not every one of you' because he knew who was going to betray him.

After washing their feet and taking his garments again, he sat down. 'Do you understand what I have done for you?' he asked. 'You call me "Master" and "Lord", and rightly so, for that is what I am. Then if I, your Lord and Master, have washed your feet, you also ought to wash one another's feet. I have set you an example: you are to do as I have done for you.'

At the end the reader says

This is the Gospel of Christ.
All   **Praise to Christ our Lord.**

▶ 15   THE SERMON

THE WASHING OF FEET
(see notes 2 and 3)

16   Silence may be kept, or A HYMN, AN ANTHEM, or A PSALM may be sung.

The washing of feet may end with this prayer.

Almighty Father,
whose Son Jesus Christ taught us
that what we do for the least of our brethren
    we do also for him:
give us the will to be the servant of others
    as he was the servant of all,

who gave up his life and died for us,
yet is alive and reigns with you and the
　　Holy Spirit,
one God, now and for ever.　**Amen.**

THE INTERCESSIONS

► 17　The form below, or a form from ASB Rite A (sections 21 or
81), or other suitable words may be used.

Silence may be kept and biddings used before each versicle
and response.

Minister　Father,
on this, the night he was betrayed, your Son
Jesus Christ washed his disciples' feet.
We commit ourselves to follow his example of
love and service.

Lord, hear us
All　　**and humble us.**

Minister　On this night, he prayed for his disciples to
be one.
We pray for the unity of your Church . . .

Lord, hear us
All　　**and unite us.**

Minister　On this night, he prayed for those who were to
believe through their message.
We pray for the mission of your Church . . .

Lord, hear us
All　　**and renew our zeal.**

Minister　On this night, he commanded them to love,
but suffered rejection himself.

We pray for the rejected and unloved . . .

Lord, hear us

All   **and fill us with your love.**

Minister   On this night, he reminded them that if the
world hated them it hated him first.
We pray for those who are persecuted for their
faith . . .

Lord, hear us

All   **and give us your peace.**

18   All may say

> **Most merciful Lord,**
> **your love compels us to come in.**
> **Our hands were unclean,**
> **our hearts were unprepared;**
> **we were not fit**
> **even to eat the crumbs from under**
> **   your table.**
> **But you, Lord, are the God of our salvation,**
> **and share your bread with sinners.**
> **So cleanse and feed us**
> **with the precious body and blood of**
> **   your Son,**
> **that he may live in us and we in him;**
> **and that we, with the whole company**
> **   of Christ,**
> **may sit and eat in your kingdom.   Amen.**

THE MINISTRY OF THE SACRAMENT

THE PEACE

▶ 19 **Stand**

The president says either of the following, or other suitable words.

> Now in union with Christ Jesus
> you who were once far off
> have been brought near
> through the shedding of Christ's blood;
> for he is our peace.

or

> Lord Jesus Christ, you said to your apostles,
> I leave you peace, my peace I give you.
> Look not on our sins but on the faith of
>   your Church,
> and grant us the peace and unity of
>   your kingdom,
> where you live and reign for ever and ever.
> **Amen.**

▶ 20 He then says

> The peace of the Lord be always with you

All **and also with you.**

THE PREPARATION OF THE GIFTS

▶ 21 The bread and wine are placed on the holy table and A HYMN may be sung.

22 This introduction may be used.

President At the eucharist we are with our
        crucified and risen Lord.
        We know that it was not only our ancestors,

but we who were redeemed
and brought forth from bondage to freedom,
from mourning to feasting.
We know that as he was with them in the
    upper room
so our Lord is here with us now.

All   **Until the kingdom of God comes**
let us celebrate this feast.

23   The president may say

Blessed are you, Lord, God of the universe,
you bring forth bread from the earth.

All   **Blessed be God for ever.**

Blessed are you, Lord, God of the universe,
you create the fruit of the vine.

All   **Blessed be God for ever.**

THE EUCHARISTIC PRAYER

THE TAKING OF THE BREAD AND CUP AND THE GIVING OF THANKS

▶ 24   The president takes the bread and cup into his hands and replaces them on the holy table.

▶ 25   The president uses one of the four EUCHARISTIC PRAYERS (pp. 101–113) with this PROPER PREFACE.

And now we give you thanks because when his hour had come, in his great love he gave this supper to his disciples, that we might proclaim his death, and feast with him in his kingdom.

THE COMMUNION

THE BREAKING OF THE BREAD AND THE GIVING OF THE BREAD AND CUP

▶ 26   THE LORD'S PRAYER is said either as follows or in its traditional form.

    President As our Saviour taught us, so we pray.
    All   **Our Father in heaven,
            hallowed be your name,
            your kingdom come,
            your will be done,
            on earth as in heaven.
            Give us today our daily bread.
            Forgive us our sins
            as we forgive those who sin against us.
            Lead us not into temptation
            but deliver us from evil.**

            **For the kingdom, the power, and the glory
              are yours
            now and for ever.   Amen.**

▶ 27   The president breaks the consecrated bread, saying

            We break this bread
            to share in the body of Christ.
    All   **Though we are many, we are one body,
            because we all share in one bread.**

28   Either here or during the distribution one of the following anthems may be said.

            **Lamb of God, you take away the sins of
              the world:
            have mercy on us.**

            **Lamb of God, you take away the sins of
              the world:
            have mercy on us.**

> Lamb of God, you take away the sins of
>   the world:
> grant us peace.

or
> Jesus, Lamb of God: have mercy on us.
> Jesus, bearer of our sins: have mercy on us.
> Jesus, redeemer of the world: give us
>   your peace.

▶ 29 Before the distribution the president says

> Draw near with faith. Receive the body of our
> Lord Jesus Christ which he gave for you, and his
> blood which he shed for you.

> Eat and drink in remembrance that he died for
> you, and feed on him in your hearts by faith with
> thanksgiving.

President The gifts of God for the people of God.
All   **Jesus Christ is holy,**
           Jesus Christ is Lord,
           to the glory of God the Father.

▶ 30 The president and people receive the Communion. Any
authorized words of distribution may be used (see p. 7).
During the distribution HYMNS and ANTHEMS may be sung.
The Alternative Service Book provision is followed for
consecration of additional bread and wine and for disposing
of what remains.

AFTER COMMUNION

31 The president may say

> Every time you eat this bread and drink this cup,
> you proclaim the death of the Lord, until he
> comes. *1 Corinthians 11.26*

32 Silence may be kept and A HYMN may be sung.

▶ 33 Either of these prayers is said.

34 President Loving Father,
we thank you for feeding us
at the supper of your Son.
Sustain us with your Spirit,
that we may serve you here on earth,
until our joy is complete in heaven
and we share the eternal banquet
with Jesus Christ our Lord. **Amen.**

or

35 President Almighty and heavenly Father,
we thank you that in this wonderful sacrament
you have given us the memorial
    of the passion of your Son Jesus Christ.
Grant us so to reverence
the sacred mysteries of his body and blood,
that we may know within ourselves
and show forth in our lives the fruits of
    his redemption;
who is alive and reigns with you and the
    Holy Spirit,
one God, now and for ever. **Amen.**

▶ 36 If THE WATCH is not kept, THIS DISMISSAL is used.

President When the disciples had sung a hymn they went
out to the Mount of Olives.
Jesus prayed to the Father, 'If it is possible, take
this cup of suffering from me'.
He said to his disciples, 'How is it that you were
not able to keep watch with me for one hour?
The hour has come for the Son of Man to be
handed over to the power of sinful men. Come,
let us go.'

Christ was obedient unto death. Go in his peace.

▶ 37   The ministers and people depart.

THE WATCH

38   If THE WATCH is to be kept there may be a procession and a hymn or psalm may be sung (see note 6).

39   The following order may be used. Silences, introduced by biddings, may follow the readings.

> John 13.16–30
> Psalm 113
>
> John 13.31–end
> Psalm 114
>
> John 14.1–14
> Psalm 115
>
> John 14.15–end
> Psalm 116.1–9
>
> John 15.1–17
> Psalm 116.10–end
>
> John 15.18–16.4a
> Psalm 117
>
> John 16.4b–15
> Psalm 118.1–9
>
> John 16.16–end
> Psalm 118.10–18
>
> John 17.1–19
> Psalm 118.19–end
>
> John 17.20–end

Then may follow Psalm 54 and the Gospel of the Watch (Lectionary p.295)

or

The Gospel of the Watch (Lectionary p.295) is read without ceremony, followed by silence.

GOOD FRIDAY

INTRODUCTION

The service for Good Friday is divided into four main parts:
(A) the Ministry of the Word, (B) the Proclamation of the Cross,
(C) the Intercessions, (D) Holy Communion. Parts A and C are
always to be used. These comprise the ASB form of
Antecommunion. Undoubtedly the central theme of any service
for Good Friday must be the cross. It is the narration of the events
leading to the crucifixion, historically from St John's Gospel,
which lies at the heart of the service. It is therefore to be
recommended that the whole of the Passion Narrative provided is
to be used on this occasion. 'They shall look on him whom they
pierced' is the climax of the portion provided to be read, and the
two optional parts, B and D, are really a dramatic and sacramental
outworking of that conclusion. It seems therefore much more
logical and effective for the Proclamation of the Cross, where it is
used, to follow the Passion Narrative, though provision is made
for it also after the Intercession, which is the more traditional
place.

There will be various ways in which the Proclamation of the
Cross is managed, according to local custom – the end should
always be the stark reality of the cross set up before the people and
an opportunity for silent reflection and intercession. For this
reason too the Intercession is much more appropriate at the foot
of the cross than at a point before the Proclamation of the Cross.

The vexed question as to whether the Holy Communion should
be celebrated on this day has been answered in the affirmative and
provision so made. It would seem that on this, above all other
days, it is wholly appropriate to eat the bread and drink the cup,
thereby proclaiming the Lord's death until he comes. However, it
is also recognized that there is a strong custom and tradition in
many churches that the eucharist should not be celebrated, but

that Holy Communion be given from the sacrament consecrated at the service of Maundy Thursday. Thus the eucharist which forms the commemoration of the Last Supper on Maundy Thursday night becomes the controlling celebration, as it were, both for the Communion in Maundy Thursday night itself and, by extension, for the Communion on Good Friday. Provision has also been made for those places where this course of action is followed.

An alternative and time-honoured custom is the practice of deliberately refraining from the sacrament on Good Friday, marking this one day out as a day of dereliction and desolation. On such a view Holy Communion would not be appropriate, following Maundy Thursday, until Easter Day.

Whilst it is perfectly possible to omit section D, thus producing what in effect would be Antecommunion, nevertheless the main thrust of the order set out in this document is that, whether the Holy Communion is celebrated or not on Good Friday, the reception of Holy Communion is to be encouraged. It is the sacramental means whereby the believer, together with the whole Church, is drawn into the movement of Christ's own self-offering to the Father, that full, perfect, and sufficient sacrifice, oblation, and satisfaction for sins of the whole world, made once and for all by the Saviour's death upon the cross.

Perhaps on this day particular attention should be drawn to those points in the service where silence is indicated. It is very much to be hoped that these silences will be carefully observed, as the meditative and reflective nature of the service greatly depends upon them. The choice of hymns and any other music will need to be selective, and sensitive to the nature of this service which should enable the believer to enter more deeply into the mystery of the finished work of Christ, his death and resurrection, and to be faced more clearly and realistically with the challenge of the crucified Lord in the world today.

NOTES

1 **Silence**   Silence is a significant part of the observance of Good
   Friday. Of the points at which such provision is made, sections 1, 2, 8
   (after the Passion), 16 (The Proclamation of the Cross), and 31 (after
   Distribution of the Holy Communion) are integral to the service. It is
   appropriate for the organ to be used only to accompany singing.

2 **Musical Texts**   Instead of the texts printed, other versions,
   traditional or modern, may be used.

3 **Hymns**   Various points are indicated for the singing of hymns; but,
   if occasion requires, they may be sung at other points also.

4 **Holy Communion**   If bread and wine are to be consecrated, ASB
   Rite A, sections 32, 36, 37, 42, and 43 are used. Eucharistic Prayer 4 is
   particularly appropriate. Alternatively the Order following the
   pattern of the Book of Common Prayer may be used (ASB Rite A,
   sections 57, 63, 65, and 69). Proper Preface 9 or 10 should be used.

5 **The Readings** (sections 4, 6, and 8)   On this day all three readings
   and the gradual psalm are to be used.

6 **The Passion Gospel** (section 8)   The Passion Gospel is announced
   'The Passion of our Lord Jesus Christ according to John' and
   concluded 'This is the Passion of the Lord'. No responses are used. It
   may be read or sung by three or more people. Afterwards silence may
   be kept.

7 **Liturgical Colour**   It is traditional for the holy table to be
   completely bare until covered by a fair linen cloth for the Ministry of
   the Sacrament (part D). Other hangings are removed. The liturgical
   colour is red.

GOOD FRIDAY

A THE MINISTRY OF THE WORD

▶ 1 The ministers enter in silence.

▶ 2 All kneel for a time of silent prayer.

▶ 3 The president stands and says THE COLLECT.

>Almighty Father,
>look with mercy on this your family
>for which our Lord Jesus Christ
>   was content to be betrayed
>   and given up into the hands of wicked men
>   and to suffer death upon the cross;
>who is alive and glorified
>   with you and the Holy Spirit,
>one God, now and for ever.   **Amen.**

▶ 4 **Sit**
OLD TESTAMENT READING

Isaiah 52.12 – 53 end TEV
The Lord says,
'My servant will succeed in his task;
he will be highly honoured.
Many people were shocked when they saw him;
he was so disfigured that he hardly looked human.
But now many nations will marvel at him,
and kings will be speechless with amazement.
They will see and understand
something they had never known.'

The people reply,
'Who would have believed what we now report?
Who could have seen the Lord's hand in this?

It was the will of the Lord that his servant
should grow like a plant taking root in dry ground.
He had no dignity or beauty
to make us take notice of him.
There was nothing attractive about him,
nothing that would draw us to him.
We despised him and rejected him;
he endured suffering and pain.
No one would even look at him –
we ignored him as if he were nothing.

But he endured the suffering that should have been ours,
the pain that we should have borne.
All the while we thought that his suffering
was punishment sent by God.
But because of our sins he was wounded,
beaten because of the evil we did.
We are healed by the punishment he suffered,
made whole by the blows he received.
All of us were like sheep that were lost,
each of us going his own way.
But the Lord made the punishment fall on him,
the punishment all of us deserved.

He was treated harshly, but endured it humbly;
he never said a word.
Like a lamb about to be slaughtered,
like a sheep about to be sheared,
he never said a word.
He was arrested and sentenced and led off to die,
and no one cared about his fate.
He was put to death for the sins of our people.
He was placed in a grave with evil men,
he was buried with the rich,
even though he had never committed a crime
or ever told a lie.

The Lord says,
'It was my will that he should suffer;

his death was a sacrifice to bring forgiveness.
And so he will see his descendants;
he will live a long life,
and through him my purpose will succeed.
After a life of suffering, he will again have joy;
he will know that he did not suffer in vain.
My devoted servant, with whom I am pleased,
will bear the punishment of many
and for his sake I will forgive them.
And so I will give him a place of honour,
a place among great and powerful men.
He willingly gave his life
and shared the fate of evil men.
He took the place of many sinners
and prayed that they might be forgiven.'

At the end the reader may say

This is the word of the Lord.

All   **Thanks be to God.**

SILENCE

▶ 5   *Psalm 22.1-22*

This response may be used.

By his wounds we have been healed.

1 My God my God   why have ǀ you for ǀ saken me:
    Why are you so far from helping me
       and from the ǀ words ǀ of my ǀ groaning?

2 My God I cry to you by day   but you ǀ do not ǀ answer:
    and by night ǀ also · I ǀ take no ǀ rest.   **R**

3 But you con ǀ tinue ǀ holy:
    you that ǀ are the ǀ praise of ǀ Israel.

4 In you our ⎪ fathers ⎪ trusted:
  they ⎪ trusted · and ⎪ you de ⎪livered them;   **R**

5 To you they cried and ⎪ they were ⎪ saved:
  they put their trust in you ⎪ and were ⎪
  not con ⎪founded.

6 But as for me   I am a worm and ⎪ no ⎪ man:
  the scorn of ⎪ men · and de ⎪spised ·
  by the ⎪ people.   **R**

7 All those that see me ⎪ laugh me · to ⎪ scorn:
  they shoot out their lips at me and ⎪ wag their ⎪
  heads ⎪ saying,

8 'He trusted in the Lord   ⎪ let him · deliver him:
  let him de ⎪liver him · if ⎪ he de ⎪lights in him.'   **R**

9 But you are he that took me ⎪ out of · the ⎪ womb:
  that brought me to lie at ⎪ peace · on my ⎪ mother's ⎪
  breast.

10 On you have I been cast ⎪ since my ⎪ birth:
  you are my God ⎪ even · from my ⎪
  mother's ⎪ womb.   **R**

11 O go not from me   for trouble is ⎪ hard at ⎪ hand:
  and ⎪ there is ⎪ none to ⎪ help.

12 Many ⎪ oxen · sur ⎪round me:
  fat bulls of Bashan close me ⎪ in on ⎪ every ⎪ side.   **R**

13 They gape ⎪ wide their ⎪ mouths at me:
  like ⎪ lions · that ⎪ roar and ⎪ rend.

14 I am poured out like water
  and all my bones are ⎪ out of ⎪ joint:
  my heart within my ⎪ breast · is like ⎪
  melting ⎪ wax.   **R**

15 My mouth is dried ⎪ up · like a ⎪ pot-sherd:
  and my ⎪ tongue ⎪ clings · to my ⎪ gums.

16 My hands and my | feet are | withered:
  and you | lay me · in the | dust of | death. **R**

17 For many dogs are | come a | bout me:
  and a band of evil | doers | hem me | in.

18 I can count | all my | bones:
  they stand | staring · and | gazing ·
    up | on me. **R**

19 They part my | garments · a | mong them:
  and cast | lots | for my | clothing.

20 O Lord do not | stand far | off:
  you are my helper | hasten | to my | aid. **R**

21 Deliver my | body · from the | sword:
  my | life · from the | power · of the | dogs;

22 O save me from the | lion's | mouth:
  and my afflicted soul from the | horns · of the |
    wild | oxen. **R**

► 6 **Sit**
NEW TESTAMENT READING (EPISTLE)

Hebrews 4.14-16; 5.7-9 NEB

Since we have a great high priest who has passed through the
heavens, Jesus the Son of God, let us hold fast to the religion
we profess. For ours is not a high priest unable to sympathize
with our weaknesses, but one who, because of his likeness to
us, has been tested every way, only without sin. Let us
therefore boldly approach the throne of our gracious God,
where we may receive mercy and in his grace find timely
help.

In the days of his earthly life Jesus offered up prayers and
petitions, with loud cries and tears, to God who was able to
deliver him from the grave. Because of his humble
submission his prayer was heard: son though he was, he
learned obedience in the school of suffering, and, once
perfected, became the source of eternal salvation for all who
obey him.

or *Hebrews 10.1-25 TEV*

The Jewish Law is not a full and faithful model of the real
things; it is only a faint outline of the good things to come.
The same sacrifices are offered for ever, year after year. How
can the Law, then, by means of these sacrifices make perfect
the people who come to God? If the people worshipping
God had really been purified from their sins, they would not
feel guilty of sin any more, and all sacrifices would stop. As it
is, however, the sacrifices serve year after year to remind
people of their sins. For the blood of bulls and goats can never
take away sins.

For this reason, when Christ was about to come into the
world, he said to God:
'You do not want sacrifices and offerings,
but you have prepared a body for me.
You are not pleased with animals burnt whole on the altar
or with sacrifices to take away sins.
Then I said, "Here I am, to do your will, O God,
just as it is written of me in the book of the Law."'
First he said, 'You neither want nor are pleased with sacrifices
and offerings or with animals burnt on the altar and the
sacrifices to take away sins.' He said this even though all these
sacrifices are offered according to the Law. Then he said,
'Here I am, O God, to do your will.' So God does away with
all the old sacrifices and puts the sacrifice of Christ in their
place. Because Jesus Christ did what God wanted him to do,
we are all purified from sin by the offering that he made of
his own body once and for all.

Every Jewish priest performs his services every day and offers
the same sacrifices many times; but these sacrifices can never
take away sins. Christ, however, offered one sacrifice for sins,
an offering that is effective for ever, and then he sat down at
the right-hand side of God. There he now waits until God
puts his enemies as a footstool under his feet. With one

sacrifice, then, he has made perfect for ever those who are purified from sin.

And the Holy Spirit also gives us his witness.
First he says,
'This is the covenant that I will make with them
in the days to come, says the Lord:
I will put my laws in their hearts
and write them on their minds.'
And then he says, 'I will not remember their sins and evil deeds any longer.' So when these have been forgiven, an offering to take away sins is no longer needed.

We have, then, my brothers, complete freedom to go into the Most Holy Place by means of the death of Jesus. He opened for us a new way, a living way, through the curtain – that is, through his own body. We have a great priest in charge of the house of God. So let us come near to God with a sincere heart and a sure faith, with hearts that have been purified from a guilty conscience and with bodies washed with clean water. Let us hold on firmly to the hope we profess, because we can trust God to keep his promise. Let us be concerned for one another, to help one another to show love and to do good. Let us not give up the habit of meeting together, as some are doing. Instead, let us encourage one another all the more, since you see that the Day of the Lord is coming nearer.

or *Hebrews 10.12-22 TEV*

Christ offered one sacrifice for sins, an offering that is effective for ever, and then he sat down at the right-hand side of God. There he now waits until God puts his enemies as a footstool under his feeet. With one sacrifice, then, he has made perfect for ever those who are purified from sin.

And the Holy Spirit also gives us his witness.
First he says,
'This is the covenant that I will make with them

in the days to come, says the Lord:
I will put my laws in their hearts
and write them on their minds.'
And then he says, 'I will not remember their sins and evil
deeds any longer.' So when these have been forgiven, an
offering to take away sins is no longer needed.

We have, then, my brothers, complete freedom to go into
the Most Holy Place by means of the death of Jesus. He
opened for us a new way, a living way, through the curtain –
that is, through his own body. We have a great priest in
charge of the house of God. So let us come near to God with
a sincere heart and a sure faith, with hearts that have been
purified from a guilty conscience and with bodies washed
with clean water.

At the end the reader may say

This is the word of the Lord.
All   **Thanks be to God.**

SILENCE

7   A CANTICLE, A HYMN, or A PSALM may be used.

▶ 8 **Stand**
THE PASSION GOSPEL
(pp. 137 and 169).

SILENCE

▶ 9 **Sit**
THE SERMON

10 A HYMN may be sung.
If THE PROCLAMATION OF THE CROSS (sections 12–18) is
not to be used, the service continues with part C, THE
INTERCESSION.

B THE PROCLAMATION OF THE CROSS

11 THE PROCLAMATION OF THE CROSS (sections 12–18) may
be used after part C.

12 A wooden cross may be brought into the church and placed
in the sight of the people.

13 Appropriate devotions follow, which may include any or all
of the following, or other suitable hymns or anthems.

14 **ANTHEM 1**

We glory in your cross, O Lord,
and praise you for your mighty resurrection;
for by virtue of your cross
joy has come into our world.

God be gracious to us and bless us:
and make his face shine upon us,
Let your ways be made known on earth:
your liberating power among all nations.
Let the peoples praise you, O God:
let all the peoples praise you.

We glory in your cross, O Lord,
and praise you for your mighty resurrection;
for by virtue of your cross
joy has come into our world.

15 **ANTHEM 2**

My people, what wrong have I done to you?
What good have I not done for you?
Listen to me.

1   I am your Creator, Lord of the universe;
I have entrusted this world to you,
but you have created the means to destroy it.

207

My people, what wrong have I done to you?
What good have I not done for you?
Listen to me.

2 I made you in my image,
     but you have degraded body and spirit
        and marred the image of your God.
     You have deserted me and turned your backs on me.

My people, what wrong have I done to you?
What good have I not done for you?
Listen to me.

3 I filled the earth with all that you need,
     so that you might serve and care for one another,
     as I have cared for you;
     but you have cared only to serve your own wealth
        and power.

Holy God,
holy and strong,
holy and immortal,
have mercy upon us.

My people, what wrong have I done to you?
What good have I not done for you?
Listen to me.

4 I made my children of one blood
     to live in families rejoicing in one another;
     but you have embittered the races
        and divided the nations.

My people, what wrong have I done to you?
What good have I not done for you?
Listen to me.

5 I commanded you to love your neighbour as yourself,
     to love and forgive even your enemies;
     but you have made vengeance your rule
        and hate your guide.

My people, what wrong have I done to you?
What good have I not done for you?
Listen to me.

6   In the fullness of time I sent you my Son,
        that in him you might know me,
        and through him find life and peace;
    but you put him to death on the cross.

Holy God,
holy and strong,
holy and immortal,
have mercy upon us.

My people, what wrong have I done to you?
What good have I not done for you?
Listen to me.

7   Through the living Christ, I called you into my Church
    to be my servants to the world,
    but you have grasped at privilege
        and forgotten my will.

My people, what wrong have I done to you?
What good have I not done for you?
Listen to me.

8   I have given you a heavenly gift
        and a share in the Holy Spirit;
    I have given you the spiritual energies
        of the age to come;
    but you have turned away
        and crucified the Son of God afresh.

My people, what wrong have I done to you?
What good have I not done for you?
Listen to me.

9   I have consecrated you in the truth;
I have made you to be one
   in the unity of the Father and the Son,
     by the power of the Spirit;
but you have divided my Church
   and shrouded my truth.

Holy God,
holy and strong,
holy and immortal,
have mercy upon us.

Turn again, my people, listen to me.

Let your bearing to one another
   arise out of your life in Christ Jesus.
He humbled himself
   and in obedience accepted the death of the cross.
But I have bestowed on him
   the name that is above every name,
   that at the name of Jesus,
   every knee should bow
   and every tongue confess,
   Jesus Christ is Lord.

Turn again, my people, listen to me.

Father, hear our prayer and forgive us.

Unstop our ears
   that we may receive the gospel of the cross.
Lighten our eyes
   that we may see your glory
   in the face of your Son.
Penetrate our minds
   that your truth may make us whole.
Irradiate our hearts with your love
   that we may love one another for Christ's sake.

Father, forgive us.

16   ANTHEM 3

You are worthy, O Christ, for you were slain;
for by your blood you ransomed men for God:
from every race and language,
    from every people and nation,
to make them a kingdom of priests
to stand and serve before our God.

**We adore you, O Christ, and we bless you,
because by your holy cross you have
    redeemed the world.**

To him who loves us
and has freed us from our sins by his blood,
and made us a kingdom of priests
to stand and serve before our God;

**To him who sits upon the throne and to the Lamb
be praise and honour, glory and might,
for ever and ever.   Amen.**

17   ANTHEM 4

**We adore you, O Christ, and we bless you,
because by your holy cross you have
    redeemed the world.**

Christ was manifested in the body,
vindicated in the spirit,
seen by angels,
proclaimed among the nations,
believed in throughout the world,
glorified in high heaven.

**We adore you, O Christ, and we bless you,
because by your holy cross you have
    redeemed the world.**

SILENCE

18   A HYMN may be sung.

C   THE INTERCESSION

▶ 19   The president introduces the prayers.

> God sent his Son into the world, not to condemn the world, but that the world might be saved through him. Therefore we pray to our heavenly Father for people everywhere according to their needs.

▶ 20   INTERCESSIONS are led by the president, or by others. The form below, or the Litany (ASB p. 99), or other suitable words may be used.

> Let us pray for the Church of God throughout the world –
> > for unity in faith, in witness and in service
> > for bishops and other ministers, and those whom they serve
> > for our bishop, and the people of this diocese
> > for all Christians in this place
> > for those to be baptized
> > for those who are mocked and persecuted for their faith
>
> that God will confirm his Church in faith, increase it in love, and preserve it in peace.
>
> SILENCE
>
> Lord, hear us.
> **Lord, graciously hear us.**
>
> Almighty and everlasting God,
> by whose Spirit the whole body of the Church
>   is governed and sanctified:
> hear our prayer which we offer
>   for all your faithful people;
> that in their vocation and ministry

212

each may serve you in holiness and truth
to the glory of your Name;
through our Lord and Saviour Jesus Christ.
Amen.

Let us pray for the nations of the world and their
leaders –
  for Elizabeth our Queen and the Parliament of
    this land
  for those who administer the law and all who
    serve in public office
  for all who strive for justice and reconciliation

that by God's help the world may live in peace
and freedom.

SILENCE

Lord, hear us.
Lord, graciously hear us.

Most gracious God and Father,
in whose will is our peace:
turn our hearts and the hearts of all to yourself,
that by the power of your Spirit
the peace which is founded on justice
may be established throughout the world;
through Jesus Christ our Lord.   **Amen.**

Let us pray for God's ancient people, the Jews,
the first to hear his word –
  for greater understanding between Christian
    and Jew
  for the removal of our blindness and bitterness
    of heart

that God will grant us grace to be faithful to his covenant and to grow in the love of his name.

Lord, hear us.
Lord, graciously hear us.

Lord God of Abraham,
bless the children of your covenant, both Jew
   and Christian;
take from us all blindness and bitterness of heart,
and hasten the coming of your kingdom,
when Israel shall be saved,
the Gentiles gathered in,
and we shall dwell together in mutual love and
peace under the one God and Father of our Lord
Jesus Christ.   **Amen.**

Let us pray for those who do not believe the
Gospel of Christ –
   for those who follow other faiths and creeds
   for those who have not heard the message
     of salvation
   for all who have lost faith
   for the contemptuous and scornful
   for those who are enemies of Christ and
     persecute those who follow him
   for all who deny the faith of Christ crucified

that God will open their hearts to the truth and
lead them to faith and obedience.

Lord, hear us.
Lord, graciously hear us.

Merciful God,
creator of all the people of the earth,

have compassion on all who do not know you,
and by the preaching of your Gospel with grace
   and power,
gather them into the one fold of the
   one Shepherd,
Christ our Lord.   **Amen.**

Let us pray for all those who suffer –
   for those who are deprived and oppressed
   for all who are sick and handicapped
   for those in darkness, in doubt and in despair,
   in loneliness and in fear
   for prisoners
   for the victims of false accusations and violence
   for all at the point of death and those who
   watch beside them.

that God in his mercy will sustain them with the
knowledge of his love.

SILENCE

Lord, hear us.
Lord, graciously hear us.

Almighty and everlasting God,
the comfort of the sad, the strength of those
   who suffer;
hear the prayers of your children who cry out of
   any trouble:
and to every distressed soul grant mercy, relief,
   and refreshment,
through Jesus Christ our Lord.   **Amen.**

Let us commend ourselves and all God's children
   to his unfailing love,
and pray for the grace of a holy life,
that, with all who have died in the peace
   of Christ,
we may come to the fullness of eternal life
and the joy of the resurrection.

Merciful Father,
accept these prayers
for the sake of your Son,
our Saviour Jesus Christ.   Amen.

21   The service may be concluded here with the form provided in part E.

D   THE MINISTRY OF THE SACRAMENT

▶ 22   The holy table is covered with a fair linen cloth.

▶ 23   If the Holy Communion is to be celebrated, the order begins at THE PREPARATION OF THE GIFTS (see note 4).

▶ 24   If Holy Communion is to be distributed the consecrated elements are placed on the holy table in silence.

▶ 25   THE LORD'S PRAYER is said either as follows or in its traditional form.

President   Let us pray for the coming of the kingdom in the words our Saviour taught us.

All   **Our Father in heaven,**
hallowed be your name,
your kingdom come,
your will be done,
on earth as in heaven.

Give us today our daily bread.
Forgive us our sins
as we forgive those who sin against us.
Lead us not into temptation
but deliver us from evil.

For the kingdom, the power, and the glory
    are yours
now and for ever.   Amen.

26   This anthem may be said.

Jesus, Lamb of God: have mercy on us.
Jesus, bearer of our sins: have mercy on us.
Jesus, redeemer of the world: give us
    your peace.

▶ 27   Before the distribution the president says

Draw near with faith. Receive the body of our
Lord Jesus Christ which he gave for you, and his
blood which he shed for you.

Eat and drink in remembrance that he died for
you, and feed on him in your hearts by faith with
thanksgiving.

Jesus is the Lamb of God
who takes away the sins of the world.
Happy are those who are called to his supper.

All   **Lord, I am not worthy to receive you,
but only say the word, and I shall be healed.**

▶ 28   The president and people receive the Communion. Any
authorized words of distribution may be used (see p. 7).
During the distribution HYMNS and ANTHEMS may be sung.
The Alternative Service Book provision is followed for
consecration of additional bread and wine and for disposing
of what remains.

▶ 29   After the distribution SILENCE is kept.

▶ 30   The service concludes with the following prayer.
      No blessing or dismissal is added.

        President   Most merciful God,
                    who by the death and resurrection of your Son
                       Jesus Christ
                    delivered and saved mankind:
                    grant that by faith in him who suffered on
                       the cross,
                    we may triumph in the power of his victory;
                    through Jesus Christ our Lord.   **Amen.**

▶ 31   The ministers depart in silence.

E   CONCLUSION

32   If there is to be no Ministry of the Sacrament, the service ends
     as follows.

▶ 33   THE LORD'S PRAYER is said either as follows or in its
     traditional form.

        President   Let us pray for the coming of the kingdom in the
                    words our Saviour taught us.
        All   **Our Father in heaven,**
                    hallowed be your name,
                    your kingdom come,
                    your will be done,
                    on earth as in heaven.
                    Give us today our daily bread.
                    Forgive us our sins
                    as we forgive those who sin against us.
                    Lead us not into temptation
                    but deliver us from evil.

                    For the kingdom, the power, and the glory
                       are yours
                    now and for ever.   Amen.

▶ 34 Either this or another suitable concluding prayer is said.
      No blessing or dismissal is added.

President   Most merciful God,
             who by the death and resurrection of your Son
                 Jesus Christ
             delivered and saved mankind:
             grant that by faith in him who suffered on
                 the cross,
             we may triumph in the power of his victory;
             through Jesus Christ our Lord.   **Amen.**

▶ 35 The ministers depart in silence.

EASTER

EASTER

INTRODUCTION

Easter Eve

According to ancient custom there is no celebration of the eucharist on Easter Eve. The orders of Morning and Evening Prayer offer adequate liturgical provision for the day, though the material on pp. 570–572 of the ASB is suitable for a service of Antecommunion. It is particularly important that Evening Prayer should be treated, by the style of its celebration, as belonging to the Eve, and not as the first service of Easter, anticipating the Easter Liturgy itself.

The Easter Liturgy

The Easter Liturgy consists of four main parts which are intended to form a single whole but may for pastoral reasons be celebrated separately: (A) the Vigil, (B) the Service of Light, (C) Baptism, (D) the Holy Communion.

A   *The Vigil*   The oldest feature of the celebration of Easter is a vigil of watching and waiting, which in early times the Church kept throughout the night, meditating on the mighty acts of God in the Scriptures and praying until dawn, when Christ's resurrection was acclaimed. Some may wish to observe a similar vigil today, either for the whole night or for just a part of it, or at least hold a short Vigil service either immediately before the Service of Light or separately at some time on Saturday evening, in preparation for the celebration of Easter Day. Others may prefer instead to begin the liturgy with the Service of Light and then to incorporate the Vigil readings into an extended Ministry of the Word (see section 18).

B   *The Service of Light*   In the Service of Light the resurrection is proclaimed in both spoken word and dramatic ceremony, the Easter candle symbolizing Christ, the light of the world, risen from the darkness of the grave. Its main feature is the joyful procession through the church, during which the light is passed progressively to all present, and it may culminate in a version of the ancient Easter Song of Praise. It is most appropriate for this service to begin in the darkness just before dawn. However, it may instead (though less suitably and dramatically) be prefixed to a later service on Easter Day, or be celebrated at an earlier hour of the night. Some may wish to prepare the candle by marking it with traditional symbolic signs at sections 7 and 8: the cross, the symbol of life and death; the first and last letters of the Greek alphabet, Alpha and Omega, a reminder that Christ is the beginning and end of all things; the numerals of the current year, a reminder that the Lord of all ages is present here and now; and five 'nails' inserted in the shape of the cross, symbolizing the wounds of Christ.

C   *Baptism*   In the early centuries of the Church's history, Baptism and Easter were intimately linked: indeed this was usually the only season in the whole year when baptisms were regularly administered. The new converts thus sacramentally entered into Christ's redeeming death and resurrection at the same time as the whole Church celebrated its memorial of those events. It is therefore most appropriate that the Easter Liturgy should include within it Baptism and/or Confirmation even if pastoral reasons require this element to be postponed until later on Easter Day. At the very least there should be the Renewal of Baptismal Vows by the congregation, as the completion of their Lenten preparation and as an affirmation of their union with Christ in his death and resurrection.

D   *Holy Communion*   The natural and proper climax of the whole Easter Liturgy is the eucharist, in which we are

sacramentally reunited with our risen Lord. This should not
be omitted, therefore, except for serious reason. The most
appropriate time for its celebration is at dawn on Easter Day.
If it is to be celebrated during the night it should be as late as
possible, preferably after midnight.

There are two main possible structures for the full Liturgy:

THE VIGIL (sections 1–2)	
THE SERVICE OF LIGHT (sections 3–17)	THE SERVICE OF LIGHT (sections 1a, 3–17)
	1b Introduction to Readings
	18 Old Testament Readings
19 Gloria in Excelsis or hymn	19 Gloria in Excelsis or hymn
20 Collect	20 Collect
21 New Testament Reading	21 New Testament Reading
22 Psalm (optional)	22 Psalm (optional)
23 The Gospel (or at section 11)	23 The Gospel (or at section 11)
24 The Sermon	24 The Sermon
THE LITURGY OF INITIATION	THE LITURGY OF INITIATION
25 Baptism and/or Confirmation (optional)	25 Baptism and/or Confirmation (optional)
26 The Renewal of Baptismal Vows	26 The Renewal of Baptismal Vows
27 Intercessions or other prayers (optional)	27 Intercessions or other prayers (optional)
THE LITURGY OF THE EUCHARIST	THE LITURGY OF THE EUCHARIST
(sections 28–47)	(sections 28–47)

NOTES

1   **The Readings** (section 48)   A wide variety has been provided,
    from which an appropriate selection may be made according to the
    length of time available. These may be presented in different ways:
    for example, dramatized or accompanied by music or visual
    illustration. Each may be followed by a suitable psalm or hymn,
    and/or prayer. A sermon may be preached after any of the readings,
    or a period of silence may be kept. It is desirable that the readings
    from Genesis 1 and Exodus 14 should always be used, and the Vigil
    may end with the reading of part or all of one of the narratives of the
    Passion (pp. 115–175). According to local circumstances, the Vigil
    may be kept in a different place from the rest of the Easter Liturgy.

2   **Lighting**   It is desirable for the building to be in darkness during
    the Vigil, except for any essential lighting. All lights should be
    extinguished at the end, or may be put out gradually during the
    reading of the Passion Narrative, where this is included. They may
    be lit again after section 17.

3   **Candles**   Small unlit candles should be distributed to members of
    the congregation either before the Vigil or before the Service of
    Light. These will be lit from the Easter Candle in the course of the
    service, and should be extinguished either after section 17, if Old
    Testament readings are to follow, or after section 20. They may be lit
    again for the Renewal of Baptismal Vows.

4   **The Lighting of the Taper** (sections 3 and 4)   Where possible, the
    ministers should go to the entrance without passing through the
    building itself. According to ancient tradition, the light for the Easter
    candle was taken from newly kindled fire and not from an already
    existing source of light. Some may wish to maintain the custom of
    lighting a bonfire outside the building and obtaining the light from
    that. If so, it is desirable for the people not to remain inside the
    building but to gather around the fire and to follow the ministers in
    the procession into the church.

5   **The Easter Candle**   This should be placed in a prominent position from Easter Day until Pentecost, and it is traditional for it to be lit at all principal services during this period. It should also be used at Baptism and may be used at Funerals throughout the year. Where a number of different congregations come together to celebrate the Easter Liturgy, only one Easter candle should be used. If it is desired to take Easter candles back to other churches, they may be lit from the first candle at the end of the service and carried in procession out of the building.

6   **The Gospel**   When this is read at section 11, it should not be accompanied by announcement or response.

7   **The Acclamation** (section 16)   This may be said or sung, and repeated as many times as desired, with gradually increasing volume.

8   **Bells and Music**   It is inappropriate for bells to be rung before the Easter Liturgy or for organ music to be used until section 19. Bells may be rung at section 19 and at the end of the service.

9   **The Renewal of Baptismal Vows**   This may also be incorporated within other services on Easter Day, in accordance with the directions on p. 275 of the ASB. When there is a Confirmation, note 12 on p. 226 of the ASB may be followed.

10   **The Blessing of the Water of Baptism**   Water for Baptism may be blessed before the Renewal of Vows (section 26). (See page 287.)

11   **A Service without Communion**   If there is no celebration of the Holy Communion, the Liturgy may end after section 26 or section 27 with the Gloria or a hymn and the Blessing and/or Dismissal from section 32, and in this case the Gloria is not used at section 19. If, alternatively, it is desired to combine the Service of Light with Morning Prayer, the Easter Anthems should follow section 16 or 17; the people should then extinguish their candles, and Morning Prayer begins immediately with the Psalms.

12   **Liturgical Colour**   White or gold.

THE EASTER LITURGY

THE VIGIL

1   The president may introduce the Vigil using these or other appropriate words.

> Brothers and sisters in Christ, on this most holy night, in which our Lord Jesus Christ passed over from death to life, the Church invites her members, dispersed throughout the world, to gather in vigil and prayer. For this is the Passover of the Lord, in which through word and sacrament we share in his victory over death.
>
> As we await the risen Christ, let us hear the record of God's saving deeds in history, recalling how he saved his people in ages past and in the fullness of time sent his Son to be our Redeemer; and let us pray that through this Easter celebration God may bring to perfection in each of us the saving work he has begun.

2   Any of the readings suggested at section 48 (with or without the accompanying psalms and prayers) or other suitable passages of Scripture may be used.

THE SERVICE OF LIGHT

▶ 3   The building being in darkness, the ministers go in silence to the main entrance, one of them carrying the unlit Easter candle.

▶ 4   All stand and face the ministers. The president lights a taper.

5   One or more of these prayers may be used.

6   Eternal God,
who made this most holy night
to shine with the brightness of your one
    true light:
set us aflame with the fire of your love,
and bring us to the radiance of your
    heavenly glory;
through Jesus Christ our Lord.   **Amen.**

7   Christ yesterday and today,
the beginning and the end,
Alpha and Omega,
all time belongs to him,
and all ages;
to him be glory and power,
through every age and for ever.   **Amen.**

8   By his holy and glorious wounds
may Christ our Lord guard and keep us.
Amen.

▶ 9   The president lights the Easter candle with the taper, saying

             May the light of Christ, rising in glory,
banish all darkness from our hearts and minds.

▶ 10   The minister bearing the candle enters the building, followed
by the other ministers, and they pause just inside the
entrance.

▶ 11   THE GOSPEL is read either here or at section 23.

▶ 12   The minister bearing the candle raises it and says or sings

             The light of Christ.
All   **Thanks be to God.**

▶ 13   The procession moves further into the building and then stops. The versicle and response are repeated, and the candles of those around are lit from the Easter candle.

▶ 14   The procession continues to the centre of the building and stops once more. The versicle and response are again repeated, and the candles of those around are lit.

▶ 15   The Easter candle is placed on a stand in the midst of the building, and all other candles in the church are now lit.

16   The minister may sav

Alleluia!   Christ is risen.
All   **He is risen indeed.   Alleluia!**

17   EXSULTET (the Easter Song of Praise) may be said or sung by a minister standing near the candle. For an alternative version see p. 287.

Rejoice, heavenly powers! Sing, choirs of angels!
Exult, all creation around God's throne!
Jesus Christ, our King, is risen!
Sound the trumpet of salvation!

Rejoice, O earth, in shining splendour,
radiant in the brightness of your King!
Christ has conquered! Glory fills you!
Darkness vanishes for ever!

Rejoice, O Mother Church! Exult in glory!
The risen Saviour shines upon you!
Let this place resound with joy,
echoing the mighty song of all God's people!

Minister   The Lord be with you
All   **and also with you.**

Minister   Lift up your hearts.
All   **We lift them to the Lord.**

230

Minister	Let us give thanks to the Lord our God.
All	**It is right to give him thanks and praise.**
Minister	It is indeed right

that with full hearts and minds and voices
we should praise you, the unseen God,
   the Father Almighty,
and your only Son, Jesus Christ our Lord,
who has ransomed us by his death,
and paid for us the price of Adam's sin.

For this is the Passover of that true Lamb of God,
by whose blood the homes of all the faithful
are hallowed and protected.

This is the night when of old you saved
   our fathers,
delivering the people of Israel from their slavery,
and leading them dry-shod through the sea.

This is the night when Jesus Christ
   vanquished hell
and rose triumphant from the grave.

This is the night when all who believe in him are
   freed from sin
and restored to grace and holiness.

Most blessed of all nights,
when wickedness is put to flight
   and sin is washed away,
lost innocence regained,
   and mourning turned to joy.

Night truly blessed,
   when heaven is wedded to earth
and all creation reconciled to God!

Therefore, heavenly Father, in the joy of
   this night,
accept our sacrifice of praise,
   your Church's solemn offering;

231

and grant that this Easter candle
may make our darkness light;
for Christ the Morning Star has risen,
never again to set,
and is alive and reigns for ever and ever.

All   **Amen.**

18   If the Vigil has not already been kept, any of the Old
Testament readings suggested in section 48 (with or without
the accompanying psalms and prayers) may be used.

▶ 19   GLORIA IN EXCELSIS is used or an appropriate HYMN.

All   **Glory to God in the highest**
and peace to his people on earth.

Lord God, heavenly King,
almighty God and Father,
we worship you, we give you thanks,
we praise you for your glory.

Lord Jesus Christ, only Son of the Father,
Lord God, Lamb of God,
you take away the sin of the world:
have mercy on us;
you are seated at the right hand of the
Father:
receive our prayer.

For you alone are the Holy One,
you alone are the Lord,
you alone are the Most High,
Jesus Christ,
with the Holy Spirit,
in the glory of God the Father.   Amen.

▶ 20   The president says THE COLLECT.

Lord of all life and power,
who through the mighty resurrection of
your Son

overcame the old order of sin and death
to make all things new in him:
grant that we, being dead to sin
and alive to you in Jesus Christ,
may reign with him in glory;
to whom with you and the Holy Spirit
be praise and honour, glory and might,
now and in all eternity. **Amen.**

▶ 21 **Sit**
NEW TESTAMENT READING (EPISTLE)

Romans 6.3-11 (see p. 270)

At the end the reader may say

This is the word of the Lord.
All **Thanks be to God.**

22 **Sit**
Psalm 118.1,16,17,22,23

This response may be used.

Alleluia! Alleluia! Alleluia!

1 O give thanks to the Lord for ╎ he is ╎ good:
his ╎ mercy · en ╎ dures for ╎ ever.

16 The right hand of the Lord does ╎ mighty ╎ things:
the right hand of the ╎ Lord ╎ raises ╎ up.

17 I shall not ╎ die but ╎ live:
and pro ╎ claim the ╎ works · of the ╎ Lord.   **R**

22 The stone that the ╎ builders · re ╎ jected:
has be ╎ come the ╎ head · of the ╎ corner.

23 This is the ╎ Lord's ╎ doing:
and it is ╎ marvel · lous ╎ in our ╎ eyes.   **R**

▶ 23   THE GOSPEL (if it has not already been read at section 11)

Matthew 28.1-10 or Mark 16.1-8 or Luke 24.1-12 (see pp. 271–273)

When it is announced

All   **Glory to Christ our Saviour.**

At the end the reader says

              This is the Gospel of Christ.
All   **Praise to Christ our Lord.**

▶ 24   THE SERMON

THE LITURGY OF INITIATION

25   BAPTISM and/or CONFIRMATION may follow (ASB pp. 229–234).

THE RENEWAL OF BAPTISMAL VOWS

26   This form or that on p. 288 may be used.

Stand
President   As we celebrate the resurrection of our Lord Jesus
              Christ from the dead, we remember that through
              the paschal mystery we have died and been
              buried with him in baptism, so that we may rise
              with him to a new life within the family of his
              Church. Now that we have completed our
              observance of Lent, we renew the promises made
              at our baptism, affirming our allegiance to
              Christ, and our rejection of all that is evil.

              Therefore I ask these questions:

              Do you turn to Christ?
All   **I turn to Christ.**

President   Do you repent of your sins?
All   **I repent of my sins.**

President	Do you renounce evil?
All	**I renounce evil.**
President	And now I ask you to make the profession of Christian faith into which you were baptized, and in which you live and grow.
	Do you believe and trust in God the Father, who made the world?
All	**I believe and trust in him.**
President	Do you believe and trust in his Son Jesus Christ, who redeemed mankind?
All	**I believe and trust in him.**
President	Do you believe and trust in his Holy Spirit, who gives life to the people of God?
All	**I believe and trust in him.**
President	This is the faith of the Church.
All	**This is our faith.** **We believe and trust in one God,** **Father, Son, and Holy Spirit.**
President	Almighty God, we thank you for our fellowship in the household of faith with all those who have been baptized in your name. Keep us faithful to our baptism, and so make us ready for that day when the whole creation shall be made perfect in your Son, our Saviour Jesus Christ. **Amen.**

27 Intercessions or other suitable prayers may be added.

THE LITURGY OF THE EUCHARIST

THE PEACE

▶ 28   The president says

> The risen Christ came and stood among his
> disciples and said, Peace be with you!
> Then were they glad when they saw the Lord.

He then says

> Alleluia!   The peace of the risen Christ be
> always with you

All   **and also with you.   Alleluia!**

29   The president may say

> Let us offer one another a sign of peace.

and all may exchange a sign of peace, greeting one another
with these words. **The Lord is risen.**   Answer   **He is
risen indeed.**

THE PREPARATION OF THE GIFTS

▶ 30   The bread and wine are placed on the holy table.

31   The president may praise God for his gifts in appropriate
words to which all respond

> **Blessed be God for ever.**

32   The offerings of the people may be collected and presented.
These words may be used.

> **Yours, Lord, is the greatness, the power,
> the glory, the splendour, and the majesty;
> for everything in heaven and on earth
>   is yours.
> All things come from you,
> and of your own do we give you.**

33   At the preparation of the gifts A HYMN may be sung.

236

THE EUCHARISTIC PRAYER

THE TAKING OF THE BREAD AND CUP AND THE GIVING OF THANKS

▶ 34 The president takes the bread and cup into his hands and replaces them on the holy table.

▶ 35 The president uses one of the four EUCHARISTIC PRAYERS (pp. 101–113) with this PROPER PREFACE.

> And now we give you thanks because you raised him gloriously from the dead. For he is the true Paschal Lamb who was offered for us and has taken away the sin of the world. By his death he has destroyed death, and by his rising again he has restored to us eternal life.

THE COMMUNION

THE BREAKING OF THE BREAD AND THE GIVING OF THE BREAD AND CUP

▶ 36 THE LORD'S PRAYER is said either as follows or in its traditional form.

President As our Saviour taught us, so we pray.
All **Our Father in heaven,**
hallowed be your name,
your kingdom come,
your will be done,
on earth as in heaven.
Give us today our daily bread.
Forgive us our sins
as we forgive those who sin against us.
Lead us not into temptation
but deliver us from evil.

For the kingdom, the power, and the glory
are yours
now and for ever.   Amen.

▶ 37   The president breaks the consecrated bread, saying

> We break this bread
> to share in the body of Christ.

All   **Though we are many, we are one body,
because we all share in one bread.**

38   Either here or during the distribution one of the following anthems may be said.

> **Lamb of God, you take away the sins of
>   the world:
> have mercy on us.**
>
> **Lamb of God, you take away the sins of
>   the world:
> have mercy on us.**
>
> **Lamb of God, you take away the sins of
>   the world:
> grant us peace.**

or   **Jesus, Lamb of God: have mercy on us.
Jesus, bearer of our sins: have mercy on us.
Jesus, redeemer of the world: give us
   your peace.**

▶ 39   Before the distribution the president says

> Draw near with faith. Receive the body of our
> Lord Jesus Christ which he gave for you, and his
> blood which he shed for you.
>
> Eat and drink in remembrance that he died for
> you, and feed on him in your hearts by faith with
> thanksgiving.
>
> Alleluia! Christ our Passover is sacrificed for us.

All   **Alleluia!   Let us keep the feast.**

▶ 40   The president and people receive the Communion. Any authorized words of distribution may be used (see p. 7).

During the distribution HYMNS and ANTHEMS may be sung.
The Alternative Service Book provision is followed for
consecration of additional bread and wine and for disposing
of what remains.

AFTER COMMUNION

41 The president may say

> Jesus said, He who eats my flesh and drinks my
> blood has eternal life, and I will raise him up at
> the last day. *John 6.54*

42 Silence may be kept and A HYMN may be sung.

▶ 43 Either or both of the following prayers is said.

44 President Heavenly Father,
you have delivered us from the power
    of darkness,
and brought us into the kingdom of your Son:
grant that, as his death has recalled us to life,
so his continual presence in us
may raise us to eternal joy. **Amen.**

45 **All** **Almighty God,
we thank you for feeding us
with the body and blood of your Son
    Jesus Christ.
Through him we offer you our souls and
    bodies
to be a living sacrifice.
Send us out
in the power of your Spirit
to live and work
to your praise and glory.   Amen.**

BLESSING AND DISMISSAL

▶ 46   President   Alleluia!   Christ is risen.
   All   **He is risen indeed.   Alleluia!**

   President   God the Father, by whose glory Christ was raised
   from the dead, strengthen you to walk with him
   in his risen life; and the blessing of God almighty,
   the Father, the Son, and the Holy Spirit, be
   among you, and remain with you always.
   Amen.

   President   Go in peace to love and serve the Lord.
   Alleluia! Alleluia!
   All   **In the name of Christ.   Alleluia! Alleluia!**

   or

   President   Go in the peace of Christ.   Alleluia! Alleluia!
   All   **Thanks be to God.   Alleluia! Alleluia!**

▶ 47   The ministers and people depart.

48   READINGS, PSALMS AND PRAYERS
   FOR THE VIGIL

I

READING

Genesis 1.1 – 2.2 (or 1.1-5, 26-end) RSV

In the beginning God created the heavens and the earth.

The earth was without form and void, and darkness was
upon the face of the deep; and the Spirit of God was moving
over the face of the waters.

And God said, 'Let there be light'; and there was light. And
God saw that the light was good; and God separated the light

from the darkness. God called the light Day, and the darkness he called Night. And there was evening and there was morning, one day.

[And God said, 'Let there be a firmament in the midst of the waters, and let it separate the waters from the waters.' And God made the firmament and separated the waters which were under the firmament from the waters which were above the firmament. And it was so. And God called the firmament Heaven. And there was evening and there was morning, a second day.

And God said, 'Let the waters under the heavens be gathered together into one place, and let the dry land appear.' And it was so. God called the dry land Earth, and the waters that were gathered together he called Seas. And God saw that it was good. And God said, 'Let the earth put forth vegetation, plants yielding seed, and fruit trees bearing fruit in which is their seed, each according to its kind, upon the earth.' And it was so. The earth brought forth vegetation, plants yielding seed according to their own kinds, and trees bearing fruit in which is their seed, each according to its kind. And God saw that it was good. And there was evening and there was morning, a third day.

And God said, 'Let there be lights in the firmament of the heavens to separate the day from the night; and let them be for signs and for seasons and for days and years, and let them be lights in the firmament of the heavens to give light upon the earth.' And it was so. And God made the two great lights, the greater light to rule the day, and the lesser light to rule the night; he made the stars also. And God set them in the firmament of the heavens to give light upon the earth, to rule over the day and over the night, and to separate the light from the darkness. And God saw that it was good. And there was evening and there was morning, a fourth day.

And God said, 'Let the waters bring forth swarms of living creatures, and let birds fly above the earth across the firmament of the heavens.' So God created the great sea monsters and every living creature that moves, with which the waters swarm, according to their kinds, and every winged bird according to its kind. And God saw that it was good. And God blessed them, saying, 'Be fruitful and multiply and fill the waters in the seas, and let birds multiply on the earth.' And there was evening and there was morning, a fifth day.

And God said, 'Let the earth bring forth living creatures according to their kinds: cattle and creeping things and beasts of the earth according to their kinds.' And it was so. And God made the beasts of the earth according to their kinds and the cattle according to their kinds, and everything that creeps upon the ground according to its kind. And God saw that it was good.]

Then God said, 'Let us make man in our image, after our likeness; and let them have dominion over the fish of the sea, and over the birds of the air, and over the cattle, and over all the earth, and over every creeping thing that creeps upon the earth.' So God created man in his own image, in the image of God he created him; male and female he created them. And God blessed them, and God said to them, 'Be fruitful and multiply, and fill the earth and subdue it; and have dominion over the fish of the sea and over the birds of the air and over every living thing that moves upon the earth.' And God said, 'Behold, I have given you every plant yielding seed which is upon the face of all the earth, and every tree with seed in its fruit; you shall have them for food. And to every beast of the earth, and to every bird of the air, and to everything that creeps on the earth, everything that has the breath of life, I have given every green plant for food.' And it was so. And God saw everything that he had made, and behold, it was very good. And there was evening and there was morning, a sixth day.

[Thus the heavens and the earth were finished, and all the host of them. And on the seventh day God finished his work which he had done, and he rested on the seventh day from all his work which he had done.]

PSALM 33.1-9

This response may be used.

The earth is filled with the loving-kindness of the Lord.

1 Rejoice in the | Lord you | righteous:
  for it be | fits the | just to | praise him.

2 Give the Lord thanks up | on the | harp:
  and sing his praise to the | lute of | ten | strings.

3 O sing him a | new | song:
  make sweetest | melody · with | shouts of | praise.   **R**

4 For the word of the | Lord is | true:
  and | all his | works are | faithful.

5 He loves | righteousness · and | justice:
  the earth is filled with the loving- | kindness |
    of the | Lord.   **R**

6 By the word of the Lord were the | heavens | made:
  and their numberless | stars · by the |
    breath of · his | mouth.

7 He gathered the waters of the sea as | in a | water-skin:
  and laid up the | deep | in his | treasures.   **R**

8 Let the whole earth | fear the | Lord:
  and let all the inhabitants of the | world | stand in |
    awe of him.

9 For he spoke and | it was | done:
  he commanded | and it | stood | fast.   **R**

243

PRAYER

Almighty God,
who wonderfully created us in your own image
and yet more wonderfully restored us
through your Son Jesus Christ:
grant that, as he came to share in our humanity,
so we may share the life of his divinity;
who is alive and reigns with you and the Holy Spirit,
one God, now and for ever.   **Amen.**

II

READING

Genesis 3 (or 3.8-13, 22-24) NEB

[The serpent was more crafty than any wild creature that the
Lord God had made. He said to the woman, 'Is it true that
God has forbidden you to eat from any tree in the garden?'
The woman answered the serpent, 'We may eat the fruit of
any tree in the garden, except for the tree in the middle of the
garden; God has forbidden us either to eat or to touch the
fruit of that; if we do, we shall die.' The serpent said, 'Of
course you will not die. God knows that as soon as you eat it,
your eyes will be opened and you will be like gods knowing
both good and evil.' When the woman saw that the fruit of
the tree was good to eat, and that it was pleasing to the eye
and tempting to contemplate, she took some and ate it. She
also gave her husband some and he ate it. Then the eyes of
both of them were opened and they discovered that they
were naked; so they stitched fig-leaves together and made
themselves loincloths.]

The man and his wife heard the sound of the Lord God
walking in the garden at the time of the evening breeze and
hid from the Lord God among the trees of the garden. But

the Lord God called to the man and said to him, 'Where are you?' He replied, 'I heard the sound as you were walking in the garden, and I was afraid because I was naked, and I hid myself.' God answered, 'Who told you that you were naked? Have you eaten from the tree which I forbade you?' The man said, 'The woman you gave me for a companion, she gave me fruit from the tree and I ate it.' Then the Lord God said to the woman, 'What is this that you have done? The woman said, 'The serpent tricked me, and I ate.'

[Then the Lord God said to the serpent:
'Because you have done this you are accursed
more than all cattle and all wild creatures.
On your belly you shall crawl, and dust you shall eat
all the days of your life.
I will put enmity between you and the woman,
between your brood and hers.
They shall strike at your head,
and you shall strike at their heel.'
To the woman he said:
'I will increase your labour and your groaning,
and in labour you shall bear children.
You shall be eager for your husband,
and he shall be your master.'
And to the man he said:
'Because you have listened to your wife
and have eaten from the tree which I forbade you,
accursed shall be the ground on your account.
With labour you shall win your food from it
all the days of your life.
It will grow thorns and thistles for you,
none but wild plants for you to eat.
You shall gain your bread by the sweat of your brow
until you return to the ground;
for from it you were taken.
Dust you are, to dust you shall return.'

The man called his wife Eve because she was the mother of all who live. The Lord God made tunics of skins for Adam and his wife and clothed them.]

He said, 'The man has become like one of us, knowing good and evil; what if he now reaches out his hand and takes fruit from the tree of life also, eats it and lives for ever?' So the Lord God drove him out of the garden of Eden to till the ground from which he had been taken. He cast him out, and to the east of the garden of Eden he stationed the cherubim and a sword whirling and flashing to guard the way to the tree of life.

PSALM 130

This response may be used.

With the Lord there is mercy.

1 Out of the depths have I called to ˈ you O ˈ Lord:
    Lord ˈ hear ˈ my ˈ voice;

2 O let your ears con ˈ sider ˈ well:
    the ˈ voice · of my ˈ suppli ˈ cation.   **R**

3 If you Lord should note what ˈ we do ˈ wrong:
    who ˈ then O ˈ Lord could ˈ stand?

4 But there is for ˈ giveness · with ˈ you:
    so that ˈ you ˈ shall be ˈ feared.   **R**

5 I wait for the Lord ★ my ˈ soul ˈ waits for him:
    and ˈ in his ˈ word · is my ˈ hope.

6 My soul ˈ looks · for the ˈ Lord:
    more than watchmen for the morning
        more I say than ˈ watchmen ˈ for the ˈ morning.   **R**

7 O Israel trust in the Lord ★ for with the ˈ Lord ·
        there is ˈ mercy:
    and with ˈ him is ˈ ample · re ˈ demption.

8   He will re∣deem ∣ Israel:
  from the ∣ multi · tude ∣ of his ∣ sins.   **R**

PRAYER

Heavenly Father,
whose blessed Son was revealed
  that he might destroy the works of the devil
and make us the children of God
and heirs of eternal life:
grant that we, having this hope,
may purify ourselves even as he is pure;
that when he shall appear in power and great glory
we may be made like him
  in his eternal and glorious kingdom;
where he is alive and reigns with you and the Holy Spirit,
one God, now and for ever.   **Amen.**

III

READING

Genesis 7.1-5, 10-18; 8.6-18; 9.8-13 RSV

Then the Lord said to Noah, 'Go into the ark, you and all
your household, for I have seen that you are righteous before
me in this generation. Take with you seven pairs of all clean
animals, the male and his mate; and a pair of the animals that
are not clean, the male and his mate; and seven pairs of the
birds of the air also, male and female, to keep their kind alive
upon the face of all the earth. For in seven days I will send
rain upon the earth forty days and forty nights; and every
living thing that I have made I will blot out from the face of
the ground.' And Noah did all that the Lord had
commanded him.

And after seven days the waters of the flood came upon the
earth. And all the fountains of the great deep burst forth, and

the windows of the heavens were opened. And rain fell upon the earth forty days and forty nights. On the very same day Noah and his sons, Shem and Ham and Japheth, and Noah's wife and the three wives of his sons with them entered the ark, they and every beast according to its kind, and all the cattle according to their kinds, and every creeping thing that creeps on the earth according to its kind, and every bird according to its kind, every bird of every sort. They went into the ark with Noah, two and two of all flesh in which there was the breath of life. And they that entered, male and female of all flesh, went in as God had commanded him; and the Lord shut him in.

The flood continued forty days upon the earth; and the waters increased, and bore up the ark, and it rose high above the earth. The waters prevailed and increased greatly upon the earth; and the ark floated on the face of the waters.

At the end of forty days Noah opened the window of the ark which he had made, and sent forth a raven; and it went to and fro until the waters were dried up from the earth. Then he sent forth a dove from him, to see if the waters had subsided from the face of the ground; but the dove found no place to set her foot, and she returned to him to the ark, for the waters were still on the face of the whole earth. So he put forth his hand and took her and brought her into the ark with him. He waited another seven days, and again he sent forth the dove out of the ark; and the dove came back to him in the evening, and lo, in her mouth a freshly plucked olive leaf; so Noah knew that the waters had subsided from the earth. Then he waited another seven days, and sent forth the dove; and she did not return to him any more.

In the six hundred and first year, in the first month, the first day of the month, the waters were dried from off the earth; and Noah removed the covering of the ark, and looked, and behold, the face of the ground was dry. In the second month, on the twenty-seventh day of the month, the earth was dry. Then God said to Noah, 'Go forth from the ark, you and

your wife, and your sons and your sons' wives with you.
Bring forth with you every living thing that is with you of all
flesh – birds and animals and every creeping thing that creeps
on the earth – that they may breed abundantly on the earth,
and be fruitful and multiply upon the earth.' So Noah went
forth, and his sons and his wife and his sons' wives with him.

Then God said to Noah and to his sons with him, 'Behold, I
establish my covenant with you and your descendants after
you, and with every living creature that is with you, the
birds, the cattle, and every beast of the earth with you, as
many as came out of the ark. I establish my covenant with
you, that never again shall all flesh be cut off by the waters of
a flood, and never again shall there be a flood to destroy the
earth.' And God said, 'This is the sign of the covenant which I
make between me and you and every living creature that is
with you, for all future generations: I set my bow in the
cloud, and it shall be a sign of the covenant between me and
the earth.'

PSALM 46

This response may be used.

The Lord of hosts is with us.

1 God is our ꟷ refuge · and ꟷ strength:
    a very ꟷ present ꟷ help in ꟷ trouble.

2 Therefore we will not fear though the ꟷ
        earth be ꟷ moved:
    and though the mountains are ꟷ shaken · in the ꟷ
        midst · of the ꟷ sea;

3 Though the waters ꟷ rage and ꟷ foam:
    and though the mountains quake at the ꟷ
        rising ꟷ of the ꟷ sea.   **R**

4 There is a river whose streams make glad the ꟷ
        city · of ꟷ God:
    the holy dwelling-place ꟷ of the ꟷ Most ꟷ High.

5 God is in the midst of her
  therefore she shall | not be | moved:
  God will | help her · and at | break of | day.   **R**

6 The nations make uproar and the | kingdoms · are|
  shaken:
  but God has lifted his | voice · and the |
  earth shall | tremble.

7 The Lord of | hosts is | with us:
  the God of | Jacob | is our | stronghold.   **R**

8 Come then and see what the | Lord has | done:
  what destruction he has | brought up|on the | earth.

9 He makes wars to cease in | all the | world:
  he breaks the bow and shatters the spear
  and burns the | chari·ots | in the | fire.   **R**

10 'Be still and know that | I am | God:
   I will be exalted among the nations
   I will be ex|alted · up|on the | earth.'

11 The Lord of | hosts is | with us:
   the God of | Jacob | is our | stronghold.   **R**

PRAYER

Almighty God,
who spoke to the prophets
that they might make your will and purpose known:
inspire the guardians of your truth,
that through the faithful witness of the few
the children of earth may be made one
    with the saints in glory;
by the power of Jesus Christ our Lord,
who alone redeemed mankind
and reigns with you and the Holy Spirit,
one God, now and for ever.   **Amen.**

IV

READING

Genesis 22.1-18 (or 22.1,2,9-13,15-18) RSV

God tested Abraham, and said to him, 'Abraham!' And he said, 'Here am I.' He said, 'Take your son, your only son Isaac, whom you love, and go to the land of Moriah, and offer him there as a burnt offering upon one of the mountains of which I shall tell you.'

[So Abraham rose early in the morning, saddled his ass, and took two of his young men with him, and his son Isaac; and he cut the wood for the burnt offering, and arose and went to the place of which God had told him. On the third day Abraham lifted up his eyes and saw the place afar off. Then Abraham said to his young men, 'Stay here with the ass; I and the lad will go yonder and worship, and come again to you.' And Abraham took the wood of the burnt offering, and laid it on Isaac his son; and he took in his hand the fire and the knife. So they went both of them together. And Isaac said to his father Abraham, 'My father!' And he said, 'Here am I, my son.' He said, 'Behold, the fire and the wood; but where is the lamb for a burnt offering?' Abraham said, 'God will provide the lamb for a burnt offering, my son.' So they went both of them together.]

When they came to the place of which God had told him, Abraham built an altar there, and laid the wood in order, and bound Isaac his son, and laid him on the altar, upon the wood. Then Abraham put forth his hand, and took the knife to slay his son. But the angel of the Lord called to him from heaven, and said, 'Abraham, Abraham!' And he said, 'Here am I.' He said, 'Do not lay your hand on the lad or do anything to him; for now I know that you fear God, seeing you have not withheld your son, your only son, from me.' And Abraham lifted up his eyes and looked, and behold, behind him was a ram, caught in a thicket by his horns; and

Abraham took the ram, and offered it up as a burnt offering instead of his son.

[So Abraham called the name of that place The Lord will provide; as it is said to this day, 'On the mount of the Lord it shall be provided.']

And the angel of the Lord called to Abraham a second time from heaven, and said, 'By myself I have sworn, says the Lord, because you have done this, and have not withheld your son, your only son, I will indeed bless you, and I will multiply your descendants as the stars of heaven and as the sand which is on the seashore. And your descendants shall possess the gate of their enemies, and by your descendants shall all the nations of the earth bless themselves, because you have obeyed my voice.'

PSALM 16.8–end

This response may be used.

In your presence is the fullness of joy.

8 I have set the Lord | always · be|fore me:
  he is at my right | hand · and I | shall not | fall.

9 Therefore my heart is glad and my | spirit · re|joices:
  my flesh | also · shall | rest se|cure.   **R**

10 For you will not give me over to the | power of | death:
  nor suffer your | faithful one · to | see the | Pit.

11 You will show me the | path of | life:
  in your presence is the fullness of joy ★ and from ⌣
    your right hand flow de|lights for |
    ever|more.   **R**

PRAYER

Almighty God,
whose chosen servant Abraham
faithfully obeyed your call

and rejoiced in your promise
that, in him, all the families of the earth should be blessed:
give us a faith like his,
that, in us, your promises may be fulfilled;
through Jesus Christ our Lord.   **Amen.**

V

READING

Exodus 14.15 – 15.1a RSV

The Lord said to Moses, 'Why do you cry to me? Tell the
people of Israel to go forward. Lift up your rod, and stretch
out your hand over the sea and divide it, that the people of
Israel may go on dry ground through the sea. And I will
harden the hearts of the Egyptians so that they shall go in
after them, and I will get glory over Pharaoh and all his host,
his chariots, and his horsemen. And the Egyptians shall know
that I am the Lord, when I have gotten glory over Pharaoh,
his chariots, and his horsemen.'

Then the angel of God who went before the host of Israel
moved and went behind them; and the pillar of cloud moved
from before them and stood behind them, coming between
the host of Egypt and the host of Israel. And there was the
cloud and the darkness; and the night passed without one
coming near the other all night.

Then Moses stretched out his hand over the sea; and the Lord
drove the sea back by a strong east wind all night, and made
the sea dry land, and the waters were divided. And the people
of Israel went into the midst of the sea on dry ground, the
waters being a wall to them on their right hand and on their
left. The Egyptians pursued, and went in after them into the
midst of the sea, all Pharaoh's horses, his chariots, and his
horsemen. And in the morning watch the Lord in the pillar
of fire and of cloud looked down upon the host of the

Egyptians, and discomfited the host of the Egyptians, clogging their chariot wheels so that they drove heavily; and the Egyptians said, 'Let us flee from before Israel; for the Lord fights for them against the Egyptians.'

Then the Lord said to Moses, 'Stretch out your hand over the sea, that the waters may come back upon the Egyptians, upon their chariots, and upon their horsemen.' So Moses stretched forth his hand over the sea, and the sea returned to its wonted flow when the morning appeared; and the Egyptians fled into it, and the Lord routed the Egyptians in the midst of the sea. The waters returned and covered the chariots and the horsemen and all the host of Pharaoh that had followed them into the sea; not so much as one of them remained. But the people of Israel walked on dry ground through the sea, the waters being a wall to them on their right hand and on their left.

Thus the Lord saved Israel that day from the hand of the Egyptians; and Israel saw the Egyptians dead upon the seashore. And Israel saw the great work which the Lord did against the Egyptians, and the people feared the Lord; and they believed in the Lord and in his servant Moses.

Then Moses and the people of Israel sang this song to the Lord.

CANTICLE

LET US SING TO THE LORD (*from Exodus 15*)

This response may be used.

> **Sing to the Lord, for he has won a glorious victory.**

1 Let us sing to the Lord
      for he has won a | glorious | victory:
      the horse and its rider he has | hurled in | to the | sea.

2 The Lord is my ǀ strength · and my ǀ song:
   he has be ǀ come ǀ my sal ǀ vation.   **R**

3 He is my God and ǀ I will ǀ praise him:
   my father's ǀ God and ǀ I · will ex ǀ alt him.

4 The Lord ǀ fights · for his ǀ people:
   the ǀ Lord ǀ is his ǀ name.   **R**

5 Your right hand Lord is ǀ glorious · in ǀ power:
   your right ǀ hand Lord ǀ shatters · the ǀ enemy.

6 Who is like you Lord ma ǀ jestic · in ǀ holiness:
   who is like you Lord
     awesome in ǀ glory ǀ working ǀ wonders?   **R**

7 In your un ǀ failing ǀ love:
   you will lead the ǀ people · you ǀ have re ǀ deemed.

8 And by your in ǀ vin · cible ǀ strength:
   you will guide them ǀ to your ǀ holy ǀ dwelling.   **R**

PRAYER

Lord God our redeemer,
who heard the cry of your people
and sent your servant Moses to lead them out of slavery:
free us from the tyranny of sin and death
and, by the leading of your Spirit,
bring us to our promised land;
through Jesus Christ our Lord.   **Amen.**

VI

READING

Deuteronomy 31.22-30 RSV

Moses wrote this song the same day, and taught it to the
people of Israel.

And the Lord commissioned Joshua the son of Nun and said, 'Be strong and of good courage; for you shall bring the children of Israel into the land which I swore to give them: I will be with you.'

When Moses had finished writing the words of this law in a book, to the very end, Moses commanded the Levites who carried the ark of the covenant of the Lord, 'Take this book of the law, and put it by the side of the ark of the covenant of the Lord your God, that it may be there for a witness against you. For I know how rebellious and stubborn you are; behold, while I am yet alive with you, today you have been rebellious against the Lord; how much more after my death! Assemble to me all the elders of your tribes, and your officers, that I may speak these words in their ears and call heaven and earth to witness against them. For I know that after my death you will surely act corruptly, and turn aside from the way which I have commanded you; and in the days to come evil will befall you, because you will do what is evil in the sight of the Lord, provoking him to anger through the work of your hands.'

Then Moses spoke the words of this song until they were finished, in the ears of all the assembly of Israel.

CANTICLE

LISTEN O HEAVENS (*from Deuteronomy 32*)

This response may be used.

I will proclaim the name of the Lord.

1 Listen O heavens and ' I will ' speak:
　　hear O ' earth the ' words · of my ' mouth.

2 Let my teaching fall like rain
　　　　and my words de'scend like ' dew:
　　like fine rain on new grass
　　　　and like ' showers on ' tender ' plants.　　**R**

3 I will proclaim the | name · of the | Lord:
  O praise the | greatness | of our | God.

4 He is the creator   his works are perfect
    and all his | ways are | just:
  a faithful God who does no wrong
    holy | righteous · and | true is | he.   **R**

PRAYER

Almighty and eternal God, sanctify and govern our hearts
and bodies in the ways of your laws and the works of your
commandments; that under your protection, now and ever,
we may be preserved in body and soul; through Jesus Christ
our Lord.   **Amen.**

VII

READING

Isaiah 54.5-14 RSV

Your Maker is your husband,
the Lord of hosts is his name;
and the Holy One of Israel is your Redeemer,
the God of the whole earth he is called.
For the Lord has called you
like a wife forsaken and grieved in spirit,
like a wife of youth when she is cast off,
says your God.
For a brief moment I forsook you,
but with great compassion I will gather you.
In overflowing wrath for a moment
I hid my face from you,
but with everlasting love I will have compassion on you,
says the Lord, your Redeemer.

For this is like the days of Noah to me:
as I swore that the waters of Noah
should no more go over the earth,

257

so I have sworn that I will not be angry with you
and will not rebuke you.
For the mountains may depart
and the hills be removed,
but my steadfast love shall not depart from you,
and my covenant of peace shall not be removed,
says the Lord, who has compassion on you.

O afflicted one, storm-tossed, and not comforted,
behold, I will set your stones in antimony,
and lay your foundations with sapphires.
I will make your pinnacles of agate,
your gates of garnet,
and all your wall of precious stones.
All your sons shall be taught by the Lord,
and great shall be the prosperity of your sons.
In righteousness you shall be established;
you shall be far from oppression, for you shall not fear;
and from terror, for it shall not come near you.

PSALM 30

This response may be used.

O Lord my God, you have made me whole.

1 I will exalt you O Lord
> for you have drawn me | up · from the | depths:
> and have not suffered my | foes to | triumph |
> over me.

2 O Lord my | God I | cried to you:
> and | you have | made me | whole.   **R**

3 You brought me back O Lord from the | land of |
> silence:
> you saved my life from among |
> those that · go | down · to the | Pit.

4 Sing praises to the Lord all | you his | faithful ones:
  and give | thanks · to his | holy | name.   **R**

5 For if in his anger is havoc
      in his good | favour · is | life:
    heaviness may endure for a night
      but | joy comes | in the | morning.

6 In my prosperity I said   'I shall | never · be | moved:
    your goodness O Lord has | set me · on so |
      firm a | hill.'   **R**

7 Then you | hid your | face from me:
    and | I was | greatly · dis|mayed.

8 I cried to | you O | God:
    and made my petition | humbly | to my | Lord.   **R**

9 'What profit is there in my blood
      if I go | down · to the | Pit:
    can the dust give you thanks |
      or de|clare your | faithfulness?

10 'Hear O | Lord · and be | merciful:
    O | Lord | be my | helper.'   **R**

11 You have turned my lamentation | into | dancing:
    you have put off my sackcloth and | girded | me with |
      joy,

12 That my heart may sing your praise and | never · be |
      silent:
    O Lord my God   I will | give you |
      thanks for | ever.   **R**

PRAYER

Almighty God,
who called your Church to witness
that you were in Christ reconciling the world to yourself:
help us so to proclaim the good news of your love,

that all who hear it may be reconciled to you;
through him who died for us and rose again
and reigns with you and the Holy Spirit,
one God, now and for ever.   **Amen.**

VIII

READING

Isaiah 55.1-11 RSV

'Ho, every one who thirsts, come to the waters;
and he who has no money,
come, buy and eat!
Come, buy wine and milk
without money and without price.
Why do you spend your money for that which is not bread,
and your labour for that which does not satisfy?
Hearken diligently to me, and eat what is good,
and delight yourselves in fatness.
Incline your ear, and come to me;
hear, that your soul may live;
and I will make with you an everlasting covenant,
my steadfast, sure love for David.
Behold, I made him a witness to the peoples,
a leader and commander for the peoples.
Behold, you shall call nations that you know not,
and nations that knew you not shall run to you,
because of the Lord your God, and of the Holy One of Israel,
for he has glorified you.

'Seek the Lord while he may be found,
call upon him while he is near;
let the wicked forsake his way,
and the unrighteous man his thoughts;
let him return to the Lord, that he may have mercy on him,
and to our God, for he will abundantly pardon.
For my thoughts are not your thoughts,

neither are your ways my ways, says the Lord.
For as the heavens are higher than the earth,
so are my ways higher than your ways
and my thoughts than your thoughts.

For as the rain and the snow come down from heaven,
and return not thither but water the earth,
making it bring forth and sprout,
giving seed to the sower and bread to the eater,
so shall my word be that goes forth from my mouth;
it shall not return to me empty,
but it shall accomplish that which I purpose,
and prosper in the thing for which I sent it.'

CANTICLE

I WILL PRAISE YOU, LORD (*from Isaiah 12*)

This response may be used.

> **Sing hymns to the Lord, for he has triumphed.**

1 I will | praise you | Lord:
   though you were angry with me
      your anger has turned away and |
      you have | comfort·ed | me.

2 Surely | God · is my | saviour:
   I will | trust and | not · be a | fraid.   **R**

3 The Lord the Lord is my | strength · and my | song:
   he has be | come | my sal | vation.

4 With joy you will | draw | water:
   from the | wells | of sal | vation.   **R**

5 Give thanks and | praise · to the | Lord:
   and | call up | on his | name.

6 Make known among the nations what | he has | done:
   proclaim that | his name | is su | preme.   **R**

7 Sing hymns to the Lord for | he has | triumphed:
   let this be made | known to | all the | world.

8 Shout aloud and sing for joy | people · of | God:
   for great in your midst is the | Holy | One of |
   Israel.   **R**

PRAYER

Lord of all power and might,
the author and giver of all good things:
graft in our hearts the love of your name,
increase in us true religion,
nourish us in all goodness,
and of your great mercy keep us in the same;
through Jesus Christ our Lord.   **Amen.**

IX

READING

Job 14.1-14 JB

Man, born of woman,
has a short life yet has his fill of sorrow.
He blossoms, and he withers, like a flower;
fleeting as a shadow, transient.
And is this what you deign to turn your gaze on,
him that you would bring before you to be judged?
Who can bring the clean out of the unclean?
No man alive!
Since man's days are measured out,
since his tale of months depends on you,
since you assign him bounds he cannot pass,
turn your eyes from him, leave him alone,
like a hired drudge, to finish his day.
There is always hope for a tree:
when felled, it can start its life again;
its shoots continue to sprout.

Its roots may be decayed in the earth,
its stump withering in the soil,
but let it scent the water, and it buds,
and puts out branches like a plant new set.
But man? He dies, and lifeless he remains;
man breathes his last, and then where is he?
The waters of the seas may disappear,
all the rivers may run dry or drain away;
but man, once in his resting place, will never rise again.
The heavens will wear away before he wakes,
before he rises from his sleep.

If only you would hide me in Sheol,
and shelter me there until your anger is past,
fixing a certain day for calling me to mind –
for once a man is dead can he come back to life? –
day after day of my service I would wait
for my relief to come.

PSALM 23

This response may be used.

> **The Lord is my shepherd: therefore can I lack nothing.**

1 The Lord ǀ is my ǀ shepherd:
    therefore ǀ can I ǀ lack ǀ nothing.

2 He will make me lie down in ǀ green ǀ pastures:
    and ǀ lead me · be ǀ side still ǀ waters.   **R**

3 He will re ǀ fresh my ǀ soul:
    and guide me in right pathways ǀ for his ǀ name's ǀ
    sake.

4 Though I walk through the valley of the ⌣
  shadow of death I will ' fear no ' evil:
 for you are with me
  your ' rod · and your ' staff ' comfort me. **R**

5 You spread a table before me
  in the face of ' those who ' trouble me:
 you have anointed my head with oil ' and my '
  cup · will be ' full.

6 Surely your goodness and loving-kindness
  will follow me ⋆ all the ' days · of my ' life:
 and I shall dwell in the ' house · of the '
  Lord for ' ever. **R**

PRAYER

Lord God,
the protector of all who trust in you,
without whom nothing is strong, nothing is holy:
increase and multiply upon us your mercy,
that you being our ruler and guide,
we may so pass through things temporal
that we finally lose not the things eternal.
Grant this, heavenly Father,
for the sake of Jesus Christ our Lord. **Amen.**

X

READING

Baruch 3.9-15, 32-end; 4.1-4 NEB

Listen, Israel, to the commandments of life; hear, and learn
wisdom. Why is it, Israel, that you are in your enemies'
country, that you have grown old in an alien land? Why
have you shared the defilement of the dead and been
numbered with those that lie in the grave? It is because you
have forsaken the fountain of wisdom. If you had walked in

the way of God, you would have lived in peace for ever. Where is understanding, where is strength, where is intelligence? Learn that, and then you will know where to find life and light to walk by, long life and peace. Has any man discovered the dwelling-place of wisdom or entered her storehouse?

Only the One who knows all things knows her: his understanding discovered her. He who established the earth for all time filled it with four-footed beasts. He sends forth the light, and it goes on its way; he called it, it feared him and obeyed. The stars shone at their appointed stations and rejoiced; he called them and they answered, 'We are here!' Joyfully they shone for their Maker. This is our God; there is none to compare with him. The whole way of knowledge he found out and gave to Jacob his servant, and to Israel, whom he loved. Thereupon wisdom appeared on earth and lived among men.

She is the book of the commandments of God, the law that stands for ever. All who hold fast to her shall live, but those who forsake her shall die. Return, Jacob, and lay hold of her; set your course towards her radiance, and face her beacon light. Do not give up your glory to another or your privileges to an alien people. Happy are we, Israel, because we know what is pleasing to God!

PSALM 19.7–end

This response may be used.

You are my strength and my redeemer.

7 The law of the Lord is perfect re | viving · the | soul:
    the command of the Lord is true |
        and makes | wise the | simple.

8 The precepts of the Lord are right ⌣
     and re|joice the | heart.
   the commandment of the Lord is pure |
     and gives | light · to the | eyes.   **R**

9 The fear of the Lord is clean and en|dures for | ever:
     the judgments of the Lord are unchanging ⌣
     and | righteous | every | one.

10 More to be desired are they than gold
     even | much fine | gold:
   sweeter also than honey ★ than the |
     honey · that | drips · from the | comb.   **R**

11 Moreover by them is your | servant | taught:
     and in keeping them | there is | great re|ward.

12 Who can know his own un|witting | sins?
     O cleanse me | from my | secret | faults.   **R**

13 Keep your servant also from presumptuous sins
     lest they get the | master·y | over me:
   so I shall be clean and | innocent · of | great of|fence.

14 May the words of my mouth and the meditation
     of my heart   be acceptable | in your | sight:
   O Lord my | strength and | my re|deemer.   **R**

PRAYER

Almighty God,
who anointed Jesus at his baptism with the
   Holy Spirit
and revealed him as your beloved Son:
inspire us, your children,
who are born of water and the Spirit,
to surrender our lives to your service,
that we may rejoice to be called the sons of God;
through Jesus Christ our Lord.   **Amen.**

XI

READING

Ezekiel 36.25-28 NEB

The Lord God says, I will sprinkle clean water over you, and
you shall be cleansed from all that defiles you; I will cleanse
you from the taint of all your idols. I will give you a new
heart and put a new spirit within you; I will take the heart of
stone from your body and give you a heart of flesh. I will put
my spirit into you and make you conform to my statutes,
keep my laws and live by them. You shall live in the land
which I gave to your ancestors; you shall become my people,
and I will become your God.

PSALM 42.1-7

This response may be used.

My soul is thirsty for the living God.

1 As a deer longs for the ∣ running ∣ brooks:
   so longs my ∣ soul for ∣ you O ∣ God.

2 My soul is thirsty for God ✱ thirsty for the ∣ living ∣
      God:
   when shall I ∣ come and ∣ see his ∣ face?

3 My tears have been my food ∣ day and ∣ night:
   while they ask me all day long ∣ 'Where now ∣
      is your ∣ God?'   **R**

4 As I pour out my soul by myself I re∣member ∣ this:
   how I went to the house of the Mighty One ∣
      into · the ∣ temple · of ∣ God.

5 To the shouts and ∣ songs of · thanks∣giving:
   a multitude ∣ keeping ∣ high ∣ festival.   **R**

6 Why are you so full of ∣ heaviness · my ∣ soul:
   and ∣ why · so un∣quiet · with∣in me?

7 O put your | trust in | God:
   for I will praise him yet
      who is my de|liver·er | and my | God.   **R**

PRAYER

Heavenly Father,
by the power of your Holy Spirit
you give to your faithful people
new life in the water of baptism.
Guide and strengthen us by that same Spirit,
that we who are born again
may serve you in faith and love,
and grow into the full stature of your Son
   Jesus Christ;
who is alive and reigns with you and the
   Holy Spirit,
one God, now and for ever.   **Amen.**

XII

READING

Ezekiel 37.1-14 JB

The hand of the Lord was laid on me, and he carried me
away by the spirit of the Lord and set me down in the middle
of a valley, a valley full of bones. He made me walk up and
down among them. There were vast quantities of these bones
on the ground the whole length of the valley; and they were
quite dried up. He said to me, 'Son of man, can these bones
live?' I said, 'You know, Lord God.' He said, 'Prophesy over
these bones. Say, "Dry bones, hear the word of the Lord.
The Lord God says this to these bones: I am now going to
make the breath enter you, and you will live. I shall put
sinews on you, I shall make flesh grow on you, I shall cover
you with skin and give you breath, and you will live; and
you will learn that I am the Lord."' I prophesied as I had been
ordered. While I was prophesying, there was a noise, a sound

of clattering; and the bones joined together. I looked, and saw that they were covered with sinews; flesh was growing on them and skin was covering them, but there was no breath in them. He said to me, 'Prophesy to the breath; prophesy, son of man. Say to the breath, "The Lord God says this: Come from the four winds, breath; breathe on these dead; let them live!"' I prophesied as he had ordered me, and the breath entered them; they came to life again and stood on their feet, a great, an immense army.

Then he said, 'Son of man, these bones are the whole House of Israel. They keep saying, "Our bones are dried up, our hope has gone; we are as good as dead." So prophesy. Say to them, "The Lord God says this: I am now going to open your graves; I mean to raise you from your graves, my people, and lead you back to the soil of Israel. And you will know that I am the Lord, when I open your graves and raise you from your graves, my people. And I shall put my spirit in you; and you will live, and I shall resettle you on your own soil; and you will know that I, the Lord, have said and done this – it is the Lord God who speaks."'

PSALM 126

This response may be used.

The Lord has done great things for us.

1 When the Lord turned again the ǀ fortunes · of ǀ Zion:
   then were we like ǀ men re ǀ stored to ǀ life.

2 Then was our mouth ǀ filled with ǀ laughter:
   and ǀ our ǀ tongue with ǀ singing. **R**

3 Then said they a ǀ mong the ǀ heathen:
   'The Lord has ǀ done great ǀ things for ǀ them.'

4 Truly the Lord has done great ǀ things for ǀ us:
   and ǀ therefore ǀ we re ǀ joiced. **R**

5 Turn again our ǀ fortunes · O ǀ Lord:
　　as the streams reǀturn · to the ǀ dry ǀ south.

6 Those that ǀ sow in ǀ tears:
　　shall ǀ reap with ǀ songs of ǀ joy.

7 He who goes out weeping 　ǀ bearing · the ǀ seed:
　　shall come again in gladness ǀ
　　　bringing · his ǀ sheaves ǀ with him.　　**R**

PRAYER

Grant, Lord,
that we who are baptized into the death
　of your Son our Saviour Jesus Christ
may continually put to death our evil desires
　and be buried with him;
that through the grave and gate of death
we may pass to our joyful resurrection;
through his merits, who died and was buried
　and rose again for us,
your Son Jesus Christ our Lord.　　**Amen**.

XIII

NEW TESTAMENT READING (EPISTLE)

Romans 6.3-11 NEB

Have you forgotten that when we were baptized into union
with Christ Jesus we were baptized into his death? By
baptism we were buried with him, and lay dead, in order
that, as Christ was raised from the dead in the splendour of
the Father, so also we might set our feet upon the new path of
life.

For if we have become incorporate with him in a death like
his, we shall also be one with him in a resurrection like his.
We know that the man we once were has been crucified with
Christ, for the destruction of the sinful self, so that we may

no longer be the slaves of sin, since a dead man is no longer answerable for his sin. But if we thus died with Christ, we believe that we shall also come to life with him. We know that Christ, once raised from the dead, is never to die again: he is no longer under the dominion of death. For in dying as he died, he died to sin, once for all, and in living as he lives, he lives to God. In the same way you must regard yourselves as dead to sin and alive to God, in union with Christ Jesus.

XIV

GOSPEL READING

Matthew 28.1-10 NEB

The Sabbath was over, and it was about daybreak on Sunday, when Mary of Magdala and the other Mary came to look at the grave. Suddenly there was a violent earthquake; an angel of the Lord descended from heaven; he came to the stone and rolled it away, and sat himself down on it. His face shone like lightning; his garments were white as snow. At the sight of him the guards shook with fear and lay like the dead.

The angel then addressed the women: 'You', he said, 'have nothing to fear. I know you are looking for Jesus who was crucified. He is not here; he has been raised again, as he said he would be. Come and see the place where he was laid, and then go quickly and tell his disciples: "He has been raised from the dead and is going on before you into Galilee; there you will see him." That is what I had to tell you.'

They hurried away from the tomb in awe and great joy, and ran to tell the disciples. Suddenly Jesus was there in their path. He gave them his greeting, and they came up and clasped his feet, falling prostrate before him. Then Jesus said to them, 'Do not be afraid. Go and take word to my brothers that they are to leave for Galilee. They will see me there.'

or *Mark 16.1-8 NEB*

When the Sabbath was over, Mary of Magdala, Mary the mother of James, and Salome bought aromatic oils intending to go and anoint Jesus; and very early on the Sunday morning, just after sunrise, they came to the tomb. They were wondering among themselves who would roll away the stone for them from the entrance to the tomb, when they looked up and saw that the stone, huge as it was, had been rolled back already. They went into the tomb, where they saw a youth sitting on the right-hand side, wearing a white robe; and they were dumbfounded. But he said to them, 'Fear nothing; you are looking for Jesus of Nazareth, who was crucified. He has been raised again; he is not here; look, there is the place where they laid him. But go and give this message to his disciples and Peter: "He is going on before you into Galilee; there you will see him, as he told you."' Then they went out and ran away from the tomb, beside themselves with terror. They said nothing to anybody, for they were afraid.

or *Luke 24.1-12 JB*

On the first day of the week, at the first sign of dawn, the women went to the tomb with the spices they had prepared. They found that the stone had been rolled away from the tomb, but on entering discovered that the body of the Lord Jesus was not there. As they stood there not knowing what to think, two men in brilliant clothes suddenly appeared at their side. Terrified, the women lowered their eyes. But the two men said to them, 'Why look among the dead for someone who is alive? He is not here; he has risen. Remember what he told you when he was still in Galilee: that the Son of Man had to be handed over into the power of sinful men and be crucified, and rise again on the third day.' And they remembered his words.

When the women returned from the tomb they told all this to the Eleven and to all the others. The women were Mary of

Magdala, Joanna, and Mary the mother of James. The other women with them also told the apostles, but this story of theirs seemed pure nonsense, and they did not believe them.

Peter, however, went running to the tomb. He bent down and saw the binding cloths but nothing else; he then went back home, amazed at what had happened.

THE EASTER SEASON

Easter Day is the Sunday of Sundays, the first day of a new creation, which extends into a season of joyful reflection on the resurrection of Jesus. The Gospel readings at the Sunday eucharist give a full place to the events associated with the resurrection, recording the appearances of the risen Lord, or the 'I am' sayings from St John understood as coming from the lips of the Lord who is already, in some sense, conqueror of death and now speaks to us from beyond the grave.

The miracle of the resurrection lies not only in the triumph of Jesus over death, but also in the inner experience of the Christian who is dead and has risen with Christ in baptism. This victory is a trailer of the final victory and redemption. Thus the Epistle readings spell out the significance of life in Christ for daily discipleship.

Pentecost, the Jewish Feast of Weeks, or Harvest, falls on the fiftieth day after Passover/Easter and marks the end of the season. A feast on the fortieth day is a memorial of the Ascension and then our thoughts are turned to anticipating the Coming of the Spirit.

The Holy Communion   The ASB provides a series of texts particularly appropriate to the season. In addition to the constantly repeated 'Alleluia' there are proper forms of the opening greeting, the introduction to the Peace, and the invitation to receive Holy Communion, and an addition to the Dismissal. There is much to be said for using these texts for the whole season, for using Gloria in Excelsis on Sundays without the Kyries, for preferring a Preface of the Resurrection daily, and for using Easter hymns until Ascension Day.

Morning and Evening Prayer   The season may be marked by a careful choice of canticles. The Easter Anthems are suitable for use throughout the season until Pentecost. If Benedictus and

Magnificat are invariably used, it would be appropriate to use Te Deum vv 1–13 and Nunc Dimittis to support them in Easter Week. For some variety until Pentecost their use could be extended to include Gloria in Excelsis and The Song of Christ's Glory. A similar selection is suitable for the shorter form of these services. The canticle 'Let us sing to the Lord' (see p. 254) is also appropriate to Easter Week.

The Easter Candle   The candle remains in its prominent place throughout the Easter season which continues until the Evening Prayer of Pentecost. It is a sign of the Risen Christ present in his Church. It should not, therefore, be ceremonially extinguished on Ascension Day. It should be lit at the Holy Communion and Morning and Evening Prayer on Sundays, and may also be lit at celebrations of the Holy Communion on other days and at Baptisms. After Pentecost it is moved to a place near the font and used at Baptisms for the remainder of the year. It may also be used for Funerals.

The Easter Garden   Although this 'visual aid' does not have the long and widespread tradition of the Crib at Christmas, there is much to be said for keeping it in a prominent place at least until the First Sunday after Easter if not until the Eve of Ascension Day.

Festivals, Holy Days, and Commemorations   From Easter Day until the First Sunday after Easter no saint's day should be observed by altering the appointed collects, psalms, and readings. The Rules to Order the Service provide for the transfer of Festivals to the following week. Nevertheless, St George's Day is a difficult problem. In addition to those parishes which bear his name there is also the connection of his day with civic and other events. While a purely ecclesiastical Festival may be transferred, it is not so easily understood in circles outside the Church when St George's Day is removed from 23 April. Accordingly we suggest that when this day occurs between Easter Day and the first Sunday after Easter, or on another Sunday after Easter, it may be sufficient to make a commemoration in the prayers of Intercession. Exceptionally the convention that there should be only one collect at Holy Communion should be relaxed and the Collect of a Martyr (ASB p. 844) used. However, where St George is the patron saint, it will often remain preferable to transfer the observance to the first free day outside Easter week.

The Rogation Days   The Monday, Tuesday, and Wednesday before Ascension Day are observed as days of prayer (Latin: *rogare*, to ask) for God's blessing on the fruits of the earth and human labour. The observance began in fifth-century France in the context of the desolation caused by earthquake, fire, and other scourges, and therefore represented the intrusion, into a season wholly given over to joy, of a foreign note of lamentation, fasting, and reparation. However, the days are still part of Eastertide. In particular the Fifth Sunday after Easter, sometimes referred to as Rogation Sunday, should be observed primarily as a festival of the Lord's resurrection.

The ASB provides proper readings and psalms for Morning and Evening Prayer together with propers for the Holy Communion (p. 884). Since Christian Aid Week sometimes coincides with the Rogation Days, the propers for Pentecost 16 (p. 713 ff), In Time of Trouble (pp. 914 ff), Social Responsibility (p. 970), or our provision for the Needs of the World (p. 290) may also be appropriately used. The alternative proper psalms and readings for St Joseph (Psalms 15,112; Genesis 1.26-33; Colossians 3.12-15,17,23,24; Matthew 13.54-end) are suitable for use on Labour Day. On any of these days the intercession at the Holy Communion might be the Litany.

From Ascension Day to Pentecost   This season of preparation for Pentecost is a time of prayer for renewal by the Holy Spirit. Hymns which call for the gift of the Holy Spirit are appropriate. On Pentecost the Renewal of Baptismal Vows may be used, and it is helpful to distribute lighted candles for ceremonies associated with this devotion.

PRAYERS FOR USE IN EASTERTIDE

1 AT AN EASTER GARDEN

Minister   The Lord has risen indeed.   Alleluia!

**All   Glory and kingship be his for ever and
           ever.   Alleluia!**

Minister   The angel said to the women, 'Do not be afraid;
           for I know that you seek Jesus who was crucified.
           He is not here; for he has risen, as he said.'
           Matthew 28.5,6

           Blessed are you, O God, the Father of our Lord
           Jesus Christ! In your great mercy you have given
           us new birth into a living hope by the
           resurrection of Jesus Christ from the dead.

           By your blessing may we who have prepared this
           garden in celebration of his victory be
           strengthened in faith, know the power of his
           presence, and rejoice in the hope of eternal glory,
           for he is alive and reigns for ever and ever.
           Amen.

           Risen Lord Jesus, as Mary Magdalen met you in
               the garden
           on the morning of your resurrection,
           so may we meet you today and every day:
           speak to us as you spoke to her;
           reveal yourself as the living Lord;
           renew our hope and kindle our joy;
           and send us to share the good news with others.
           Amen.

**All   Dying you destroyed our death,
           rising you restored our life.
           Lord Jesus, come in glory.**

2 ON THE EVENING OF EASTER DAY

O Lord,
who by triumphing over the power of darkness
prepared our place in the new Jerusalem:
grant that we, who have this day
    given thanks for your resurrection,
may praise you in the city where you are
    the light;
for there with the Father and the Holy Spirit
you live and reign, now and for ever.   **Amen**.

3 AN INTERCESSION

Minister   Father, we praise you for the resurrection of
your Son Jesus Christ from the dead.
Shed his glorious light on all Christian people
that we may live as those who believe in the
triumph of the cross.

Lord, hear us.

All   **Lord, graciously hear us.**

Minister   We pray for those who at this season are
receiving in baptism your Son's new life by
water and the Spirit . . .
Dying with Christ, may they know the power of
his resurrection.

Lord, hear us.

All   **Lord, graciously hear us.**

Minister	We pray for all whom we know and love, both near and far . . . May their eyes be opened to see the glory of the risen Lord. Lord, hear us.
All	**Lord, graciously hear us.**
Minister	We pray for those who suffer pain and anguish . . . Grant them the faith to reach out towards the healing wounds of Christ and be filled with his peace. Lord, hear us.
All	**Lord, graciously hear us.**
Minister	We remember before you those who have died in the hope of the resurrection . . . Unite us with them in your undying love. Lord, hear us.
All	**Lord, graciously hear us.**
Minister	Join our voices, we pray, Lord our God, to the songs of all your saints in proclaiming that you give us the victory through Jesus Christ our Lord.
All	**Amen.**

4 THANKSGIVING FOR THE RESURRECTION

Minister	Let us bless the Father, the Son, and the Holy Spirit; let us praise and exalt him for ever.
All	**Blessing and honour and glory and power be to him who sits upon the throne and to the Lamb for ever and ever.**

**Great and marvellous are your works, Lord
  God Almighty;
just and true are your ways, King of saints;
all glorious your gifts, Spirit of life.**

**Blessing and glory and wisdom and
thanksgiving and honour and power and
might be to our God for ever and ever.
Amen.**

O give thanks to the Lord, for he is gracious:
and his mercy endures for ever.

He has loved us from all eternity:
for his mercy endures for ever.

And remembered us when we were in trouble:
for his mercy endures for ever.

For us men and for our salvation he came down
  from heaven:
for his mercy endures for ever.

He became incarnate of the Virgin Mary by the
  power of the Holy Spirit, and was made man:
for his mercy endures for ever.

By his cross and passion he has redeemed
  the world:
for his mercy endures for ever.

And has washed us from our sins in his
  own blood:
for his mercy endures for ever.

On the third day he rose again:
for his mercy endures for ever.

And has given us the victory:
for his mercy endures for ever.

He ascended into heaven:
for his mercy endures for ever.

And opened wide for us the everlasting doors:
for his mercy endures for ever.

He is seated at the right hand of the Father:
for his mercy endures for ever.

And ever lives to make intercession for us:
for his mercy endures for ever.

Glory to the Father, and to the Son,
and to the Holy Spirit:
as it was in the beginning, is now,
and shall be for ever.   Amen.

For the gift of his Spirit:
Blessed be Christ.

For the catholic Church:
Blessed be Christ.

For the means of grace:
Blessed be Christ.

For the hope of glory:
Blessed be Christ.

For the triumphs of his gospel:
Blessed be Christ.

For the lives of his saints:
Blessed be Christ.

In joy and in sorrow:
Blessed be Christ.

In life and in death:
Blessed be Christ.

Now and to the end of the ages:
Blessed be Christ.

Minister	Blessing and honour and thanksgiving and praise more than we can utter, more than we can conceive, be to you, O most adorable Trinity, Father, Son, and Holy Spirit, by all angels, all people, all creatures, for ever and ever.
All	**Amen and Amen.**

SUPPLEMENTARY TEXTS

SUPPLEMENTARY TEXTS

KYRIE ELEISON (see General Note 10)

This may be said in any of the following forms.

Lord, have mercy.
Lord, have mercy.

Christ, have mercy.
Christ, have mercy.

Lord, have mercy.
Lord, have mercy.

Lord, have mercy.	Kyrie eleison.
Lord, have mercy.	**Kyrie eleison.**
Lord, have mercy.	Kyrie eleison.
Christ, have mercy.	**Christe eleison.**
Christ, have mercy.	Christe eleison.
Christ, have mercy.	**Christe eleison.**
Lord, have mercy.	Kyrie eleison.
Lord, have mercy.	**Kyrie eleison.**
Lord, have mercy.	Kyrie eleison.

Lord, have mercy upon us.
Lord, have mercy upon us.
Lord, have mercy upon us.

Christ, have mercy upon us.
Christ, have mercy upon us.
Christ, have mercy upon us.

Lord, have mercy upon us.
Lord, have mercy upon us.
Lord, have mercy upon us.

or alternatively the following may be used when there are no Prayers of Penitence.

IN LENT

Minister	Lord, we have sinned against you: Lord, have mercy.
All	**Lord, have mercy.**
Minister	Lord, show us your mercy and love.
All	**And grant us your salvation.**
Minister	May almighty God have mercy on us, forgive us our sins, and bring us to everlasting life.
All	**Amen.**

AFTER EASTER

Minister	You raise the dead to life in the Spirit: Lord, have mercy.
All	**Lord, have mercy.**
Minister	You bring pardon and peace to the sinner: Christ, have mercy.
All	**Christ, have mercy.**
Minister	You bring light to those in darkness: Lord, have mercy.
All	**Lord, have mercy.**

TRISAGION

Holy God,
holy and strong,
holy and immortal,
have mercy upon us.

ALTERNATIVE FORM OF THE EASTER SONG OF PRAISE

This alternative version of the Easter Song of Praise may be sung to a tune of metre 10.10.10.10, such as 'Woodlands'. If this version is used, the whole of the section beginning 'The Lord be with you' (p. 230) may be said first, followed by these sung stanzas.

Sing choirs of heaven! Let saints and angels sing!
Around God's throne exult in harmony!
Now Jesus Christ is risen from the grave!
Salute your king in glorious symphony!

Sing choirs of earth! Behold, your light has come!
The glory of the Lord shines radiantly!
Lift up your hearts, for Christ has conquered death!
The night is past; the day of life is here!

Sing church of God! Exult with joy outpoured!
The gospel trumpets tell of victory won!
Your Saviour lives: he's with you evermore!
Let all God's people shout the long Amen!

FORM FOR THE BLESSING OF THE WATER OF BAPTISM

The president stands before the water of baptism and says

Praise God who made heaven and earth,
All **who keeps his promise for ever.**

President Almighty God, whose Son Jesus Christ
was baptized in the river Jordan:
we thank you for the gift of water
to cleanse us and revive us;
we thank you that through the waters of the
Red Sea, you led your people out of slavery
to freedom in the promised land;
we thank you that through the deep waters
of death you brought your Son, and raised
him to life in triumph.

287

Bless this water, that your *servants* who *are*
  washed in it may be made one with Christ
  in his death and in his resurrection,
  to be cleansed and delivered from all sin.
Send your Holy Spirit upon *them* to bring
  them to new birth in the family of your
  Church, and raise *them* with Christ to full
  and eternal life.
For all might, majesty, authority, and power
  are yours, now and for ever. **Amen.**

ALTERNATIVE FORM FOR
THE RENEWAL OF BAPTISMAL VOWS

President   As we celebrate the resurrection of our Lord Jesus
Christ from the dead, we remember that through
the paschal mystery we have died and been
buried with him in baptism, so that we may rise
with him to a new life within the family of his
Church. Now that we have completed our
observance of Lent, we renew the promises made
at our baptism, affirming our allegiance to
Christ, and our rejection of all that is evil.

Therefore I ask these questions:

Do you turn to Christ?

All   **I turn to Christ.**

President   Do you repent of your sins?
All   **I repent of my sins.**

President   Do you renounce evil?
All   **I renounce evil.**

President   Let us now proclaim the Christian faith into
which we were baptized and in which we live
and grow.

Do you believe and trust in God the Father, who made the world?

All **I believe in God, the Father almighty, creator of heaven and earth.**

President Do you believe and trust in his Son, Jesus Christ, who redeemed mankind?

All **I believe in Jesus Christ, his only Son, our Lord.**
He was conceived by the power of the Holy Spirit
and born of the Virgin Mary.
He suffered under Pontius Pilate,
was crucified, died, and was buried.
He descended to the dead.
On the third day he rose again.
He ascended into heaven,
and is seated at the right hand of the Father.
He will come again to judge the living and the dead.

President Do you believe and trust in the Holy Spirit, who gives life to the people of God?

All **I believe in the Holy Spirit,**
the holy catholic Church,
the communion of saints,
the forgiveness of sins,
the resurrection of the body,
and life everlasting.   Amen.

President This is the faith of the Church.
All **This is our faith.**
We believe and trust in one God,
Father, Son, and Holy Spirit.

President Almighty God, we thank you for our fellowship in the household of faith with all those who have

been baptized in your name. Keep us faithful to
our baptism, and so make us ready for that day
when the whole creation shall be made perfect in
your Son, our Saviour Jesus Christ.   **Amen.**

THE NEEDS OF THE WORLD

The following material is suitable for services in Christian
Aid Week, One World Week, and similar occasions relating
to world development.

OPENING SENTENCE

May the gracious favour of the Lord our God be upon us:
prosper the work of our hands. (Alleluia) *Psalm 90.17*

or

The earth is the Lord's and all that is in it: the compass of the
world and those who dwell therein. (Alleluia) *Psalm 24.1*

COLLECTS Rogation 2 and 3 (ASB pp. 884–885)

PSALMS 65 or 65.8-end; 67; 145.3-9 or 145.10-16

READINGS

Job 28; Isa 58.1-9; Joel 2.21-26

2 Cor 9.6-15; James 4.13 – 5.11; 1 John 3.14-18;
1 John 4.16-21

Matt 6.19-24; Matt 25.31-end; Luke 16.19-end; John 6.1-14.

PROPER PREFACE Of the Resurrection (14)

POSTCOMMUNION SENTENCE

Remember the words of the Lord Jesus, 'It is more important
to give than to receive.' (Alleluia) *Acts 20.35*

A LECTIONARY

NOTES

1   The lectionary is a single course. The options marked A, B, and C may be used in one of two ways:
    (i) Any of the three options may be used consistently in any year.
    (ii) The three options may be used in a three-year cycle.
    (iii) The short gospels provided for Monday, Tuesday, and Wednesday in Holy Week are a single option. If the longer alternative is chosen, it should be preferred on each day so that the entire passion narrative is read.

2   The readings provided for the Holy Communion may be used at Morning and Evening Prayer or Night Prayer.

3   Two New Testament readings are provided at the Holy Communion for each day in Easter Week. The readings from Acts correspond to the Daily Eucharistic Lectionary (ASB pp. 1071–91), where they continue after Easter 1. These Acts readings may be used in place of those from Exodus or in place of those from 1 Peter.

4   On some other days (Easter Day, the First Sunday after Easter, Ascension Day, the Sunday after Ascension, and Pentecost) there is also provision for those who wish to use a New Testament Reading before the Epistle at Holy Communion.

5   **The Passion Readings on Palm Sunday**   The readings recommended in the lectionary include the accounts of the Agony, the Trial, and the Crucifixion. If it is desired, they may be expanded to include the Anointing, the Preparation, the Last Supper, and the Burial.
    A Matthew 26 and 27
    B Mark 14 and 15
    C Luke 22 and 23

    If, for serious pastoral need, the readings are shortened, or at an additional celebration of the Holy Communion, the following may be read:
    A Matthew 27.1-54
    B Mark 15.1-39
    C Luke 22.66 – 23.49

A LECTIONARY

Morning Prayer	The Holy Communion	Evening Prayer	Night Prayer

ASH WEDNESDAY

Ps 102
Dan 9.3-19
1 Tim 6.6-19
	Isa 58.1-8
	  or Joel 2.12-17
	  or Amos 5.6-15
	Ps 51.1-17
	
	1 Cor 9.24-end
	  or 2 Cor 5.20-6.2
	  or Jas 4.1-10
	
	Matt 6.1-6, 16-18
	  or Matt 6.16-21
	  or Luke 18.9-14
	
	During the Imposition
	of Ashes Psalms 6 and 90
	may be used.
		Ps 38
		Isa 1.11-20
		Matt 16.21-end
			Ps 90
			Ezek 18.21-22,
			  30b-end
			  or any reading from
			  those provided for the
			  Holy Communion

On the Seventh Sunday before Easter, in Year 2, any of the Old Testament readings provided here, especially Ezek 18.21-22, 30b-end, may be substituted for the Old Testament reading at Holy Communion (Num 15.32-36).

PALM SUNDAY

Ps 61,62 Zech 9.9-12 John 12.12-19,44-end	*Palm ceremony* A Matt 21.1-11 B Mark 11.1-10 C Luke 19.29-40 *The Holy Communion* Isa 50.4-9a Ps 69.1-3,7-9,21-23 Phil 2.5-11 A Matt 26.36-27.54 B Mark 14.32-15.39 C Luke 22.39-23.49	Ps 86 or Ps 22.1-22 Isa 5.1-7 A Matt 21.12-43 B Mark 11.11-12.12 C Luke 19.41-20.18	Ps 55 Zech 12.8,10

MONDAY IN HOLY WEEK

Ps 41 Lam 1.1-12a A John 14 B Gal 6.11-end C John 14.1-14	Isa 42.1-7 Ps 27.1-3,16-end Heb 9.11-14 John 12.1-11 or A Mark 14.1-31 B Luke 22.1-38 C Matt 26.1-30	Ps 25 Lam 2.8-19 A Gal 6.11-end B John 14 C John 14.15-end	Ps 71 A Heb 2.9-end B Heb 2.9-end C Gal 6.11-end

Morning Prayer	The Holy Communion	Evening Prayer	Night Prayer

TUESDAY IN HOLY WEEK

Ps 27	Isa 49.1-6	Ps 69.1-16	Ps 73
Lam 3.1-18	Ps 71.1-6,15-17	Lam 3.40-51	A Heb 8.1-6
or 3.1-30		A Eph 2.11-18	B Heb 8.1-6
A John 15.1-17	Heb 9.24-end	B John 15–16.4a	C Eph 2.11-18
B Eph 2.11-18		C John 15.18–16.4a	
C John 15.1-17	John 13.21-33,		
	36-38 or		
	A Mark 14.32-end		
	B Luke 22.39-65		
	C Matt 26.31-end		

WEDNESDAY IN HOLY WEEK

Ps 31	Isa 50.4-9a	Ps 88	Ps 102
Wisdom 1.16 – 2.11,	Ps 69.17-23,32-35	Isa 63.1-9	A Phil 3.7-11
21-29 or		A 1 Cor 1.18-25	B Phil 3.7-11
Jer 11.18-20	1 Pet 2.9-end	B John 16.4b-end	C 1 Cor 1.18-25
A John 16.4b-end		C John 16.16-end	
B 1 Cor 1.18-25	Matt 26.14-25 or		
C John 16.1-15	A Mark 15.1-39		
	B Luke 22.66–23.48		
	C Matt 27.1-54		

MAUNDY THURSDAY

Ps 39	*Blessing of the oils*	Ps 42; 43	Ps 54
Exod 11	Isa 61.1-9	Lev 16.2-24	A Luke 22.31-65
John 17	Ps 89.19-30; 133	A Luke 22.3-28	B Matt 26.30-end
		B Matt 26.17-29	C Mark 14.26-end
	Jas 5.13-16a	C Mark 14.12-42	Night Prayer is not
	or Rev 1.5b-8		said if the Watch is
			observed.
	Luke 4.16-21		
	The Lord's Supper		
	Exod 12.1-8,11-14		
	Ps 116.11-end		
	1 Cor 11.23-29		
	John 13.1-15		
	The Watch		
	A Luke 22.31-62		
	B Matt 26.30-end		
	C Mark 14.26-end		

GOOD FRIDAY

Ps 40	Isa 52.12–53-end	Ps 130;143.1-11	Ps 140.1-8,12-end
Gen 22.1-18	Ps 22.1-22	Lam 5.15-end	A Luke 23.50-end
A Luke 22.66–23.49		Col 1.15-23 or	B Matt 27.55-61
B Matt 27.1-54	Heb 4.14-16,5.7-9	A Luke 23.50-end	C Mark 15.40-end
C Mark 15.1-39	or 10.1-25	B Matt 27.55-61	or Col 1.15-23
	or 10.12-22	C Mark 15.40-end	
	John 18 and 19		
	or 18.1–19.37		

Morning Prayer	The Holy Communion	Evening Prayer	Night Prayer
EASTER EVE			
Ps 142 Hosea 6.1-6 Matt 27.62-end	*Antecommunion* Job 14.1-14 Ps 57 1 John 5.5-12 John 2.18-22	Ps 116 Job 19.21-27 1 Pet 3.17-end	Ps 30 Phil 2.5-11
THE EASTER LITURGY			
	Gen 1.1-5,26-end Ps 33.1-9 Exod 14.15-15.1a Exod 15.1b-3,6,11,13 Other readings from section 48 of the Easter Liturgy may be included. Rom 6.3-11 Ps 118.1,16-17,22-23 A Matt 28.1-10 B Mark 16.1-8 C Luke 24.1-12		
EASTER DAY			

Ps 113;114;117
Isa 43.16-21
1 Cor 15.12-20
	Acts 10.34-43
	Ps 118.14-24
	Col 3.1-4
	
	or Exod 14.15-22
	    Easter Anthems
	    Rom 6.3-11
	
	or Isa 12
	    Te Deum 8-13
	    Rev 1.10-18
	
	John 20.1-10 or
	A Matt 28.1-10
	B Mark 16.1-8
	C Luke 24.1-12
		Ps 118
		Song of Solomon
		  3.2-5;8.6-7
		John 20.1-23
		  or 20.10-23
			Ps 115
			1 Cor 5.6-8

MONDAY IN EASTER WEEK			

Ps 120;121
Isa 25.1-9
Acts 13.26-41
	See note 3
	Exod 12.14-36
	Easter Anthems
	  or Acts 2.14,22–32
	    Ps 16.1-6
	1 Pet 1.3-9
	
	Matt 28.8-15
		Ps 122;123
		Song of Solomon
		  2.8-end
		Matt 28.16-end
			Ps 2
			Rom 8.9-11

Morning Prayer	The Holy Communion	Evening Prayer	Night Prayer

TUESDAY IN EASTER WEEK

Ps 124;125	Exod 12.37-end	Ps 126;127	Ps 23
Isa 26.1-19	Ps 16.8-end	Micah 7.7-end	Heb 13.20-21
John 20.1-10		Phil 1.19-26	
	or Acts 2.36-41		
	Ps 33.1-5		
	1 Pet 1.10-12		
	John 20.11-18		

WEDNESDAY IN EASTER WEEK

Ps 128;129	Exod 13.1-16	Ps 130;131	Ps 93
Isa 42.10-16	Ps 111	1 Kings 17.17-end	2 Cor 5.14-17
Luke 24.1-12		1 Thess 4.13-end	
	or Acts 3.1-10		
	Ps 105.1-9		
	1 Pet 1.13-21		
	Luke 24.13-35		

THURSDAY IN EASTER WEEK

Ps 132	Exod 13.17–14.14	Ps 133;134	Ps 111
Isa 61	Ps 114	Zech 8.1-8	Eph 2.4-10
Acts 5.27-32		Col 3.1-11	
	or Acts 3.11-end		
	Ps 8		
	1 Pet 2.1-10		
	Luke 24.36-49		

FRIDAY IN EASTER WEEK

Ps 135	Exod 14.15-end	Ps 136	Ps 113
Jer 31.1-14	Ps 116.1-9	Zeph 3.14-end	Rom 14.7-9
Rev 7.9-end		Acts 17.16-31	
	or Acts 4.1-12		
	Ps 118.14-24		
	1 Pet 4.1-6		
	John 21.1-14		

SATURDAY IN EASTER WEEK

Ps 137.1-6;138	Exod 15.1-21	Ps 139	Ps 16
Ezek 37.1-14	Ps 116.11-end	Job 14.1-14	1 Cor 15.20-22
Mark 16.1-8		Acts 26.1-23	
	or Acts 4.13-21		
	Ps 118.14-24		
	1 Pet 4.7-11		
	Mark 16.9-15		

LECTIONARY

Morning Prayer	The Holy Communion	Evening Prayer	Night Prayer

FIRST SUNDAY AFTER EASTER

Morning Prayer	The Holy Communion	Evening Prayer	Night Prayer
Ps 115	Exod 15.1-11	Ps 34	Ps 48
	Ps 30.1-5,11-end		2 Tim 1.8-10
Year 1		*Year 1*	
Deut 11.1-15	or Acts 3.1-10	Exod 16.1-15	
2 Cor 4.5-end	Ps 145.1-12	John 6.24-51	
Year 2	1 Pet 1.3-9	*Year 2*	
Deut 4.25-end	or 1 John 5.1-5	Isa 51.1-16	
Rev 2.1-11		1 Cor 15.20-28,53-end	
	John 20.19-29		

ASCENSION EVE

Morning Prayer	The Holy Communion	Evening Prayer	Night Prayer
		Ps 93;99	Ps 98
		Ezek 1.4-5,22-end	Heb 10.12-14
		or Song of the Three Children 29-37	
		Col 2.20-3.4	

ASCENSION DAY

Morning Prayer	The Holy Communion	Evening Prayer	Night Prayer
Ps 96;97	Dan 7.13-14	Ps 15;24	Ps 8
2 Sam 23.1-5	Ps 21.1-7	Isa 52.7-12	Eph 2.4-10
Heb 1.1-2.4	Acts 1.1-11	Heb 2.5-end	
	or Acts 1.1-11		
	Ps 47		
	Eph 1.15-end		
	A Matt 28.16-end		
	B Mark 16.14-end		
	C Luke 24.45-end		

SUNDAY AFTER ASCENSION

Morning Prayer	The Holy Communion	Evening Prayer	Night Prayer
Ps 108;110	2 Kings 2.9-15	Ps 138;150	Ps 146
Isa 65.17-end	Ps 24	Dan 7.9-14	Phil 2.5-11
or Jer 31.1-14		or 2 Kings 2.1-15	
John 17.1-13	or Acts 1.12-14	A Luke 24.45-end	
(14-end)	Ps 68.1-6,18-20	B Matt 28.16-end	
		C Mark 16.14-end	
	Eph 4.7-8,11-13		
	A Mark 16.14-end		
	B Luke 24.45-end		
	C Matt 28.16-end		

PENTECOST EVE

Morning Prayer	The Holy Communion	Evening Prayer	Night Prayer
		Ps 145	Ps 143.1-11
		Deut 16.9-15	Isa 11.1-3
		John 7.37-39	

Morning Prayer	The Holy Communion	Evening Prayer	Night Prayer

PENTECOST

Ps 68.1-20	Acts 2.1-11	Ps 104 or	Ps 48
Gen 11.1-9	Ps 36.5-10	104.1-5,26-end	2 Cor 1.21-22
or Ezek 37.1-14		Joel 2.21-end	
Rom 8.1-17	or Exod 19.16-end	Rom 8.18-27	
	Ps 122		
	Acts 2.1-11 or		
	1 Cor 12.4-7,12-13		
	John 20.19-23		
	or 14.15-26		

READINGS FOR A DEVOTION ON THE WAY OF THE CROSS

Introduction   Mark 8.34

1	1 Pet 2.21-23	Ps 2.1-6	Matt 27.20-26
2	1 Pet 2.24	Ps 45.1-7	Mark 15.16-20a; John 19.17
3	Heb 2.14-18	Ps 109.20-end	Mark 10.38-40
4	Lam 2.13	Ps 35.11-19	Luke 2.33-35
5	Phil 3.8-11	Ps 73.23-end	Mark 15.21
6	2 Cor 4.7-11	Ps 27.9-end	Matt 25.31-40
7	Isa 53.3-5	Ps 88.15-end	Matt 11.28-30
8	Isa 53.6-7	Ps 130	Luke 23.27-31
9	Isa 63.2,3a,5	Ps 69.1-4,13-16	John 12.23-24
10	Col 2.13-15	Ps 22.1-11,18-19	Mark 15.22-24
11	Gal 2.19-20	Ps 43	Luke 23.33-34a
12	Phil 2.5-11	Ps 31.1-18	Luke 23.44-46
13	2 Cor 1.5-7	Ps 88.10-14	Luke 23.50-53a
14	Rom 6.3-4	Ps 16.7-end	Luke 23.53b-56a
15	Song of Solomon 3.2-5;8.6-7	Ps 139	John 20.1-10

READINGS FOR A DEVOTION ON THE SEVEN WORDS FROM THE CROSS

Introduction   Zech 12.10;13.1

1	Isa 53.4-end	Ps 51.10-17	Luke 23.32-34
2	Rom 8.31-end	Ps 16.7-end	Luke 23.39-43
3	2 Cor 5.16-19	Ps 85.8-end	John 19.26-27
4	Heb 5.7-9	Ps 22.1-22	Mark 15.34
5	Isa 55.1-11	Ps 42 and 43	John 19.28-29
6	Isa 63.1-9	Ps 40	John 19.30
7	Phil 1.20-23	Ps 31	Luke 23.46

Conclusion   Rev 1.5b-7

COPYRIGHT

Lent, Holy Week, Easter: Services and Prayers
Copyright © The Central Board of Finance of the Church of
England, 1984, 1986

Texts for Local Use

ACKNOWLEDGEMENTS

Thanks are due to the following for permission to reproduce copyright material:

The Church of the Province of South Africa: extracts from *Ash Wednesday to Easter* (William Collins Sons and Co. Ltd.)

William Collins Sons & Co. Ltd: psalms from *The Psalms: A New Translation for Worship* (The Liturgical Psalter) © 1976, 1977 English text David L. Frost, John A. Emerton, Andrew A. Macintosh, all rights reserved, © pointing 1976, 1977 William Collins Sons & Co. Ltd.

International Committee on English in the Liturgy: excerpts from the English translation of the Roman Missal © 1973 International Committee on English in the Liturgy Inc. Altered with permission.

A.R. Mowbray and Co. Ltd: extracts from *The Office of Compline – An Alternative Order*, © David Silk 1980; material from *Prayers for Use at the Alternative Services*, compiled and adapted by David Silk, © David Silk 1980; 'A Thanksgiving for the Resurrection' (adapted) from *Cambridge Offices and Orisons* edited by E. Milner-White and B.T.D. Smith.

Biblical passages are reproduced with permission from

The Revised Standard Version of the Bible (RSV), copyright 1946, 1952 © 1971, 1973 by The Division of Christian Education of the National Council of the Churches of Christ in the USA.

The New English Bible (NEB), © 1961, 1970 Oxford and Cambridge University Presses.

The Jerusalem Bible (JB), © 1966 by Darton, Longman & Todd Ltd and Doubleday and Company Inc.

Today's English Version (TEV), © American Bible Society 1966 1971, 1976. British usage edition *Good News Bible* published 1976 by The Bible Societies and Collins.

Those who prepared these services wish to record their indebtedness to The Book of Common Prayer According to the Use of the Episcopal Church of the USA (1979).